REVELATIONS:
BOOK I

St. Bridget of Sweden

Translated by: D.P. Curtin

REVELATIONS

Copyright @ 2008 Dalcassian Publishing Company

All rights reserved. No part of this publication may be reproduced, distributed, or transmitted in any form or by any means, including photocopying, recording, or other electronic or mechanical methods, without the prior written permission of the publisher, except in the case of brief quotations embodied in critical reviews and certain other non-commercial uses permitted by copyright law. For permission request, write to Dalcassian Publishing Company at dalcassianpublishing at gmail.com

ISBN: 979-8-8692-7502-8 (Paperback)

Library of Congress Control Number:
Author: Curtin, D.P. (1985-)

Printed by Ingram Content Group, 1 Ingram Blvd, La Vergne, Tennessee

First printing edition 2008.

REVELATIONS

REVELATIONS

Prologue

1- Astonishment and wonders were heard in our land. Indeed, it was wonderful that Moses, a zealot for the law, should hear a fiery law for the vengeance of sinners from the midst of the fire of God's jealousy. But it is more astonishing that today the humble and meek in spirit hear the voice of Jesus Christ, God and man, just as Helias once heard in his thin ear.

2- For he who, in the zeal of his justice, first brought the most hard, ignorant, and rude people into subjection to his law through fear, now, in his gentleness and mercy, arranges to bring the people, trained in both the old and new laws, into subjection through love. For the spirit of the great terror of God had preceded, overthrowing the mountains of the proud and crushing the rocks of hardened hearts, and shaking with penitence, stirring minds to salvation, and the fire of divine love, glowing in the gospel of Christ by the most evident signs of his great love for his people, who gave himself up for them in death , that they themselves should not die eternally, and their own people should betray themselves to him for his glory, so that I may speak in a certain way.

3- In this fire God appeared, not according to the excellence of his divinity, but according to the humble condition of our servitude, in which he redeemed the world. And now follows the hissing of the mildness of the divine mercy, inviting all, because of the prayers and merits of the mother of mercy, the virgin Mary, from the depths of sin to the breeze of the most placid mercy. And in this aura the Lord, to whom it is proper to be merciful, manifests the omnipotence of his divinity in the sublimest of compassion, so that all may be inexcusable, by the apparent divine judgment, who have despised the mercy so gently and sweetly shown.

4- Or is he not inexcusably worthy of being struck by the justice of the divine judgment, who, with such sweet words and deeds as the series of this revelation contains, despises and rejects the mercy offered to him?

5- Wherefore let them prepare all their hearts, and expand all the recesses of their wills, that a good measure of mercy, that is, heaped up above merit, stirred above hope, overflowing above desire and all thought, may be poured out through the mediator of God and men from his Son, namely the source of all piety.

6- And I have no suspicion that a deluded spirit steals these legends from the minds. For it is not to be believed that an evil spirit either deceives the truly righteous, or converts sinners for the better, or infuses cold hearts with charity which he does not have or promotes the glory of God in someone whom he envies.

7- For just as it is impossible for the spirit of truth either to speak lies, or to turn anyone away from justice, or to inspire pride and envy in the hearts of those subject to it, or to bring contempt of Almighty God, so the opposites of these evils to the spirit of falsity are completely forbidden because of their innate malice and wickedness.

8- Or if anyone contends that these, or any of these good things, are possible for an evil spirit to do, it follows that he grants that the opposites of these things are possible for a good and holy spirit. And an inevitable error will come, so that evils will be attributed to God and good things to the devil, and the devil will be believed to be the ruler and ruler of the righteous, but God will be blasphemed as the supporter and instigator of the wicked.

9- That if anyone wishes to discern the truly just, lest he be deceived by false justice, let him know that from the truly just are banished: first, all truly evil things, in so far as they work to eternal death, namely, lust, covetousness, and pride; then also false goods, viz., virtue vainly boasting to itself, or cowardly to defend justice, or burning with bitter jealousy to judge others, so that in justice he may be humble from virtue, steadfast from humility, calm from stability of mind.

10- Wherefore the truly righteous man neither complains of his own glory, lest by this he be deceived by the devil, nor shrinks from the defense of justice through cowardice, so that by this means he may be overcome by the malice of men, nor succumbs to disturbances of any kind, so that the state of his mind may be overthrown by fierce impatience from the foundation of right reason.

11- For no one is righteous in this, because a disturbance of mind befalls him, if, however, the disturbance does not drive him away from patience and the foundation of the other virtues. Wherefore also Christ, when he had said to the Father out of sadness and confusion in the agony of his mind: "Remove this cup from me!", showing that that confusion had not diverted his mind from the foundation of virtues, he added: "Not as I will, but as thou wilt."

12- And this can be noted no less than what was said above in the pre-alleged figure. For a great spirit is vainglory, which overthrows all the eminence of virtues, which is in the manner of a monk, and all constancy, which is like the firmness of rocks. And the terror of threats and persecutions will move hearts, so that they yield to the importunities of men.

13- And the fire of jealousy burns in the righteous, not yet perfected in the power of patience and meekness, against sinners, as is evident in the Pharisee, who boasted of his righteousness, and raged with the fire of indignation against the publican, as did Simon against Magdalene. But the Lord is not in such ferocity, and therefore room is given to the devil to tempt and deceive.

14- They are not to be suspected of such a bride of Christ, whom he chose for himself in this kind of grace. Who, while still living in marriage, brought her husband to the perfection of continence, so that they lived together for many years without exaction or repayment of the conjugal debt. And now, still bound by marriage, she preferred a widow's sobriety in diet and dress. And by the earnestness of his heart and prayers, he foretold a great perfection of religion and grace in that future.

15- And when she was now freed from the law of her husband, distributing her goods to her heirs and the poor, and freeing herself from the nets of the world, and following the poor poor Christ, she retained nothing but the simplest subsistence and contemptible clothing. Because of this, Christ visited her, who had rejected all the consolations of the world, with surprising consolations and graces.

16- In all of which, complaining not of his own glory but of God's, he would indeed have preferred to be guarded on the side out of humility, except as to the salvation of his neighbors, he was commanded to manifest himself to certain persons through the command of the spirit, or rather of Christ, appearing to him in the spirit. And he wished to accumulate the glory of Christ by his reproaches and insults. By truth, meekness, and justice, expressing in himself the form of Christ's life, he suffered injury gratuitously and with impunity, even from the smallest and the meanest persons.

17- Who would think that such a life should be exposed to the mockery of the demons, and would dare to accuse Christ of so much impiety, that he would not protect him who hoped in him, and glorified not himself but himself from the fullness of his love? Or does a good husband expose a chaste and faithful spouse to be mocked by an adulterer?

REVELATIONS

18- Therefore let the rashness of foolish judgment give way, and place be given to the glory and grace of God, who is known to be so much greater, the more incredible it seems to us in our ignorance and modest faith. For who, except by the grace of the same Spirit, will be able to believe that Christ, residing in heaven, speaks to a woman who still lives in this mortality?

19- But just as we have received from the words of Christ himself, when mountains and forests are looked upon, the sky seems close to their eminence, although it is not, so also Christ, reigning in heaven, may be seen close by spiritual vision, however removed from his bodily presence he may be. Such a distant local vision cannot be prejudiced.

20- O truly astonishing and admirable appearance and grace, and certainly to be revealed to every nation that is under heaven, by which Christ, so gravely injured by the atrocities of the Christians, that hardly any remnant of the seed of justice can be found, shows mercy to the ungrateful and entices the guilty to beg for forgiveness!

21- Of course, this apparition is more astonishing than that one, by which he showed himself in the flesh. She devoured the surface of the flesh with carnal eyes, this one devours God and man with spiritual eyes.

22- Through her he spoke to mortals that he would die, through her he spoke to those who will die forever, that they may become immortal. Through her walking on earth he showed the divine in the human, through her reigning in heaven he reconciled the human to the divine.

23- In that debt he paid in justice by dying for us, in this debt he promises to give us sinners a gift of mercy.

24- I say, this wonderful apparition is so astonishing that it is scarcely possible to believe and comprehend the power of so great a miracle by the small capacity of the human heart. For although reason itself finds the truth full of power in the very words and works which are heard in this apparition and are proved by experience, yet the weakness itself does not grasp what reason says to grasp the words of the audience and the benefits of experience.

25- For even I myself, who have written this, although I am most assured of the truth of this spirit through words and deeds, yet I hardly understand what I judge to be worthy of all acceptance. Not to mention that I think that all the listeners could believe this, who had not heard the words and did not know the works.

26- Just as it is said of the resurrection of Christ, that it was shown little by little through many evidences, because the frail breasts of mortals could not contain all the newness of the miracle at the same time, so I believe Christ will do in this miracle: in the long course of time to make the greatness of the miracle known by many evidences of virtues, than the eyes the sinners of the heart, accustomed to darkness, cannot suddenly recognize it.

27- This, however, should prepare the minds of all for an easier acceptance of the truth, that so many words and so many miracles preach no other faith than that which Christ preached. They do not bring us a new Christ, but the same one who suffered for us.

28- They take nothing from the truth that is in Christ or add to it, but by mercy, which is shown in them so much more abundantly, as the misery of sinners is now known to be greater than what ever was.

29- Let us therefore give thanks to the Father of mercies and to the God of quick consolation, who, in so many miseries of the aging world, meets with so many mercies to the poor, lest they slip into the abyss of despair.

30- For he who will soberly and faithfully pay attention to the words of the present book, which are few in comparison to the many, will not be able to doubt that the words - not of him who is empty of power, but of him who is full of power, of truth - could not have been spoken except by the spirit of truth.

31- He who wishes to prove his works must find reliable witnesses, with whom he can verify the truth of his works, if he wishes.

32- Now the beginning of this revelation was made to the aforesaid lady, transmitted to me, who prefaced this prologue, that I might make it known to others, thus assumed by Christ:

33- "The devil sinned threefold, namely, pride, because I created him well, greed, with which he aspired to be not only my equal but also superior, and pleasure, with which he was so delighted with the glory of my divinity, that he would have gladly killed me, if he had been able, to take my place And because of this, falling from heaven, he filled the world with these three sins and violated the human race through them.

34- For this reason I assumed man and came into the world, that by my humility I might annihilate his pride, and by my poverty I might destroy his desire. And I suffered the most severe penalty of the cross, in order to exterminate his abominable concupiscence and to open heaven to man with the blood of my heart and my death, closed by his sins, if he wishes, as much as is in him, to work for this.

35- But now the men of the kingdom of Sweden, especially that class of men which is called courtly or military, are sinning, as the devil sinned before. For they are proud of the beautiful bodies which I have given them. They are going around the divisions, which I did not want to give them. They fall into such abominable concupiscence that, if it were possible for them, they would rather kill me than be deprived of their pleasures, or endure my terrible judgment, which threatens them for their sins.

36- And therefore those bodies, of which they are proud, shall be slain by sword, lance, and axe. Those beautiful limbs, of which they boast, will be torn by beasts and birds. The goods which they collect against my will, strangers will plunder and they themselves will need.

37- But because of their abominable pleasures they displease my Father so much that he does not deign to admit them to the vision of his face. And because they would willingly kill me if they could, they themselves will be delivered to the hells into the hands of the devil, to be killed by him with eternal death.

38- And I would have carried this judgment long before the kingdom of Sweden had it not been for the prayers of my friends who are among them, who incline me to mercy. And therefore the time will come when I will gather my friends to myself, so that they will not see the evils that I will bring over to them in the kingdom. However, some of my friends will then live and see the culmination of their merits.

39- Now, therefore, because kings and princes and prelates do not want to recognize me from my favors, so that they may come to me, I will gather the poor, the weak, the young, and the pitiful persons, with whom I will fill their places, lest there be any deficiency in my army because of their absence."

40- And when the person to whom this revelation was made groaned and complained that the judgment was too harsh, the Lord added: "As long as a man lived, the access to the heavenly kingdom was open to him. If they knew how to change their lives, I knew how to moderate the sentence."

41- But the works that occur at the present time, confirming the present truth, are as follows: First, that one ignorant woman proposes this, which she does not want to imagine, since she is of noble and proven life, living in humility and widowhood and, if she wanted, she would not know or to confine the least, since it is the most simple and tame.

42- The second thing is that the scribe of these, being the most religious and the most simple, unwilling for any reason to put his hand to writing, considering himself, on account of his ignorance, less fit for such a work, was constrained by the fear of death from Christ, and almost died, until he consented; and the agreement having been made, he suddenly took care of the failure of the time.

43- The third thing is that a demoniac in Osgocia, in the presence of two reliable witnesses, was cleansed at the words of the mouth of the aforesaid religious, the form of which this woman heard from Christ and the brother said to the demon according to the command of Christ.

44- The fourth is that another demoniac in Sweden, in the presence of three reliable witnesses, was cleansed in the same way by the same religious.

45- The fifth is the conversion of one public harlot by the blessing of the Blessed Virgin, appearing with Christ as Lord.

46- The sixth is the conversion of several great men in the kingdom, who at a time and place have with one voice experienced the movement of their hearts for the better; if they had not been displeased with Christ, they would confess that it was done by him at his words sent by him.

Chapter 1 begins the first book of the heavenly revelations of God.

The words of our Lord Jesus Christ to his chosen beloved bride concerning the certification of his most excellent incarnation and the improbation of the profanation and breaking of our faith and baptism and how he invites the aforesaid beloved bride to his beloved.

1- I am the creator of heaven and earth, one in the Godhead with the Father and the Holy Spirit, I who spoke to the prophets and patriarchs and whom they were waiting for. Because of their desire and according to my promise, I assumed flesh without sin and concupiscence, entering the virgin bowels like the sun shining through the most pure stone. For just as the sun does not hurt the glass when it enters, so the Virgin's virginity was not corrupted in the assumption of my humanity.

2- But I thus assumed flesh, that I might not forsake divinity. And I was not inferior in deity with the Father and the Holy Spirit, ruling and filling all things, although I was in the womb of a virgin with humanity. For as brightness is never separated from fire, so my divinity is never separated from humanity, even in death.

3- Then I wanted to tear the body itself, most clean from sin, for the sins of all, from the sole of the foot to the top of the foot, and nail it to the cross. Even this is sacrificed on the altar every day, so that man may love me so much more and remember my benefits more often.

4- But now I am completely forgotten and neglected and despised and like a king expelled from his own kingdom, in whose place the worst thief has been elected and honored.

5- Finally, I wanted my kingdom to be in man, and over him I should be king and lord by right, because I made him and redeemed him. But now he has broken and profaned the faith which he promised me in baptism, he has violated and despised my laws which I proposed to him. He loves his own will and deigns to listen to me. Moreover, he exalted the worst thief, the devil, over me and gave him his faith.

6- He who is truly a thief, because he snatches to himself the soul of man, which I have redeemed with my own blood, by suggesting evil and promising lies. And therefore, he seizes, as if he were more powerful than I, since I am so powerful that I can do all things by word, so just, that even if all the saints asked, I would not do the least thing against justice. But since man, given free will, willingly consents to the devil's contemptuous commandments, it is therefore just that man should experience his tyranny.

7- Because the devil himself, having been made good by me, but falling by his evil will, is as it were mine to avenge the evil. But though I am just so despised, yet I am so merciful, that whoever has sinned against my mercy and humbled himself, I will forgive them what they have committed, and I will deliver them from the unjust robber.

8- But those who have persisted in my contempt, I will visit upon them my justice in such a way that the hearers will tremble and those who experience it will say: 'Woe, because we were ever born and conceived, woe, because we ever provoked the Lord of majesty to anger!'

9- And you, my daughter, whom I have chosen for me and with whom I speak with my spirit, love me with all your heart, not like a son and daughter or parents, but more than anything in the world! Because I, who created you, spared no member of mine to be put to death for you. And I still love your soul so charitably that, before I lose it, I would once more, if it were possible, nail it to the cross for it.

10- To imitate my humility, because I, the king of glory and of angels, was clothed in cheap clothes, I stood naked at the pillar, I heard all the reproaches and mockery with my ears.

11- Let me put my will before yours, because my mother, your lady, from the beginning to the end never wanted anything but what I wanted. If you do this, then your heart will be with my heart and will be inflamed with my love, just as something dry is easily ignited by fire. Your soul will be filled with me, and I will be in you, so that everything temporal will become bitter to you, all the pleasure of the flesh as poison.

12- You will rest in the arms of my deity, where there is no pleasure of the flesh but joy and delight of the spirit. When the soul is pleased with this, it is inwardly and outwardly full of joy, and does not think or desire anything but the joy it has.

13- So love me alone, and you will have everything you want, and you will abound. Is it not written that the oil of the widow did not fail until the Lord gave rain upon the earth according to the word of the prophet? I am a true prophet. If you believe in my words and fulfill them, you will not lack oil and joy and exultation forever."

Chapter 2

The words of our Lord Jesus Christ to the daughter, already taken as his bride, about the true articles of faith and what are the ornaments and signs and the will that the bride should have with respect to the bridegroom.

1- I am the creator of heaven and earth, the sea, and all that is in them. I am one with the Father and the Holy Spirit, not like gods of stone or gold, as was once said, nor many, as was then thought, but one God, the Father and the Son and the Holy Spirit, triune in persons, one in substance, creating all things and from created by nothing, immutable and omnipotent, remaining without beginning and without end.

2- It is I who was born of a virgin, not losing my divinity but associating it with humanity, so that in one person I might be the true son of God and the son of a virgin. I am the one who was nailed to the cross and died and was buried, remaining unharmed by the deity. Because although I died in humanity and in the flesh, which I, the only Son, assumed, I still lived in the Godhead, in which I was one God with the Father and the Holy Spirit.

3- I am the same, who rose from the dead and ascended into heaven, who even now speaks with you with my spirit. I chose you and chose you to be my bride, to show you my secrets, because it pleases me so.

4- You indeed became mine by a certain right, when at the death of your husband you entrusted your will into my hands, when you even thought of him when he died and asked how you could be poor for me, and you wanted to leave everything for me. And therefore, by right, you became mine. And it was necessary for me to provide you with such charity. Therefore, I take you to be my bride and my own pleasure, such as God should have with a chaste soul.

5- It therefore belongs to the bride to be ready when the bridegroom wishes to perform the nuptials, so that she is decently adorned and clean. Then you are well cleansed, if your thoughts are always about your sins, how I cleansed you in baptism from the sin of Ade, whenever I supported and supported you when you fell into sins.

6- The bride must also bear the marks of her bridegroom on her breast, that is to pay attention to the favors and works that I have done for you, namely, how nobly I created you, giving you body and soul, how nobly I enriched you, giving you health and temporal things, how sweetly I brought you back, since I died for you and restored your inheritance, if you wish to have it.

7- The bride must also follow the will of the bridegroom. What is my will, except that you wish to love me above all things, to wish nothing else but me? I created all things for man's sake and subjected all things to him, but he loves all things more than me and hates nothing but me. I bought him again his inheritance, which he had lost, but he was so alienated and turned away from reason, that he preferred that transitory honor, which is nothing but the foam of the sea, rising like a mountain in a moment, and quickly sinking to naught, then the eternal honor in which it is a perpetual good.

8- But you, my bride, if you miss nothing but me, if you despise everything for me, not only children and parents, but also honors and judgments, I will give you the most precious and sweetest reward. I will give you not gold and silver but myself as a bridegroom and premium, who am a king to glory.

9- But if you are ashamed to be poor and despised, consider that your God precedes you, whom your relatives and friends have left on earth, because you did not seek earthly friends, but heavenly ones. But if you fear and fear the weight of labor and weakness, consider how great it is to burn in the fire!

10- What would you have gained if you had encountered a temporal master like me? For I, though I love you with all my heart, yet do not act contrary to justice in one point, lest, as you have transgressed in all members, so you may be satisfied in all.

11- However, because of the good will and the purpose of making amends, I change justice into mercy, remitting heavier punishments for a small amendment.

12- Therefore, willingly embrace a little work, so that you may arrive at a great premium sooner! For it is fitting that the bride should be tired with labors with the bridegroom, so that she may rest with him more faithfully."

Chapter 3

The words of our Lord Jesus Christ to the bride concerning the information of love and honor of the bridegroom to the bridegroom himself and of the hatred of the wicked to God and love to the world.

1- I am your God and the Lord whom you worship. I am the one who supports the heavens and the earth by my power, and they are not supported by some other things or pillars. I am the one who, under the guise of bread, sacrifices daily on the altar a true God and a true man. I am the one who chose you.

2- Honor my Father! Love me! Obey my Spirit! Take my mother as your mistress! Honor all my saints! Observe the right faith, which he will teach you, who, having experienced in himself the conflict of two spirits, that is, of falsehood and of truth, with my help, has condemned him!

3- Keep true humility! What is true humility but to give praise to God for the good things given?

4- But now many hate me and regard my deeds and words as pain and vanity, but they embrace and love the adulterer, that is, the devil. For whatever they do for me is with grumbling and bitterness. Nor would they acknowledge my name, unless they were confused by the fear of men.

5- But they love the world so sincerely that they do not tire night and day in its work and are always fierce in its love. I am pleased with the slaughter of these men, as if a man were to give money to his enemy for the purpose of having his son killed.

6- They do so themselves. For they give me small alms and honor me with their lips, so that worldly prosperity may succeed them, and they may remain in their honor and sin. Wherefore their good spirit is killed by their excelling in good.

7- But if you wish to love me with all your heart and desire nothing but me, I will draw you to me through love, as a magnet, that is, a stone, attracts iron to itself, and I will place you in my arm, which is so strong that no one can reach out. so rigid that no one can touch it when stretched out. It is also so sweet that it overcomes all spices and has no comparison with the pleasures of the world."

8- This was a certain holy man, a master in theology, who was called Master Mathias of Sweden, a canon of Lincoln. Who glossed the whole Bible excellently. And he was tempted by the devil in a very subtle way about many heresies against the Catholic faith, all of whom he rejected with the help of Christ, and he could not be overcome by the devil, as this is more clearly contained in the legend of the life of Lady Bridget.

9- And this teacher Mathias composed the prologue to these books, which begins "Awe and miracles," etc. He was a holy man and spiritually powerful in work and word.

10- When he died in Sweden, the bride of Christ, then staying in Rome, he heard a voice in his spirit saying thus: "O blessed art thou, teacher Mathias, for the crown which has been fashioned for thee in heaven. Come now, therefore, to wisdom, which will never end!"

Chapter 4

The words of our Lord Jesus Christ to the bride, how she should not be afraid of being revealed by him, nor think that they are evil spirits. And about the doctrine of knowing a good or an evil spirit.

1- I am your creator and redeemer. Why were you afraid of my words? And why did you think about what spirit they were in, good or bad? Tell me, what did you find in my words that your conscience did not tell you to do? Or have I commanded you something contrary to reason?"

2- To which the bride replied: "No way, but all that is true and I was badly mistaken." The spirit or the bridegroom answered: "I commanded you three things, by which you could know the good spirit. I commanded you to honor your God, who made you, and gave you all that you have. This tells you, for your reason, to honor him above all things.

3- I ordered you to keep the right faith, that is, to believe that without God nothing has been done, without God nothing can be done.

4- I commanded you to love the reasonable continuity of all things, because the world was made for the sake of man, so that man may use it as necessary. Thus, you can know the unclean spirit by three things, opposite to these.

5- For he advises you to complain of your own praise and to be proud of what has been given to you. He also advises you to be unfaithful. He also suggests to you the incontinence of all members and of all things, and to this his heart is inflamed.

6- He also sometimes deceives under the guise of good. That is why I have commanded you to always discuss your conscience and open it to spiritual sages.

7- Therefore, do not doubt then that the spirit of God is good with you, when you long for nothing else but God and are all fired up about him. I alone can do this, and it is impossible for the devil to approach you. But neither can he approach any evil person, unless he is permitted by me, either because of sins or because of some secret judgment known to me, because he is my creature, like everything else, and he was made good by me, but he is evil in his malice and therefore I am lord over him.

8- That is why some impute a false fault to me, who say that those who seek me out of excessive devotion are said to be mad and possessed by demons. They make me like a man who, having a chaste wife, and trusting well in her husband, supposes her to be an adulterer. Such would be if I were to let a man, who had just an attitude of charity towards me, be given over to the devil.

9- But because I am faithful, the soul of no one who devoutly serves me will be dominated by a demon. And though sometimes my friends appear as if they were mad, yet this is not because of the passion of the devil, nor because they turn away from me out of fervent devotion, but because of a failure of the brain, or because of some other hidden cause, which they have for their humiliation.

10- It can even happen sometimes that the devil takes power from me over the flesh of good men to reward them or that he overshadows their consciences, but he can never have dominion over the souls of those who have faith and pleasure in me.

Chapter 5

The words of the greatest love of Christ to the bride in the wonderful figure of the noble castle, by which the church is designated as a warrior, and how the church of God will be rebuilt again through the glorious prayers of the Virgin and the saints.

1- I am the creator of all, I am the king of glory and the lord of the angels. I founded for myself a noble castle and placed in it my chosen ones.

2- The foundation of which my enemies pierced and prevailed upon my friends to such an extent that the marrow came out of the feet of my friends, when they were bound by the wood, that is, the cypress.

3- Their mouths are crushed with stones, and they are tormented by hunger and thirst. Moreover, they also pursue their master. Now my friends cry out for help with groans, justice cries out for vengeance, but mercy says to spare."

4- Then God himself said to the heavenly army that was standing by: "What do you think of these who occupied my castle?"

5- They all answered as if with one voice: "Lord, in you is all justice and in you we see all things. You, existing without beginning and without end, Son of God, all judgment is given to you, you are their judge."

6- And he said: "It is true that you know and see everything in me, yet for the sake of this bride who is standing, pronounce a just judgment!" And they said: "This is justice, that those who broke down the wall should be punished as thieves, and those who persist in malice should be punished as trespassers, and those who were captives should be freed and the hungry fed."

7- Then spoke the mother of God, Mary, silent in the voice of the former, saying: "My Lord and my dearest son, you were in my womb a true God and man. You sanctified me, who was an earthly vessel, by your condescension. I beg you: have mercy on them once more!"

8- Then the Lord answered the mother: "Blessed be the word of your mouth! This is like the sweetest fragrance rising up to the deity. You are the glory of the angels and of all the saints and the queen, because by you the deity is comforted and all the saints are happy. And because your will was from the beginning Your youth was like mine, so I will do what you want once more."

9- And to the army he said: "Because you have fought manfully, therefore because of your charity I will appease you. Behold, I will rebuild my wall because of your prayers."

10- I will save and heal those who have been oppressed by force, and I will honor them a hundredfold for the insults they have suffered. But to the violent, if they ask for mercy, I will give peace and mercy. But those who despised me will feel my justice."

11- Then he said to the bride: "My bride, I have chosen you and brought you into my spirit. You hear my words and those of my saints, who, although they see everything in me, have nevertheless spoken for your sake, so that you may understand, because you, who you are still in the flesh, cannot see into me like these who are spirits.

12- Now I will show you what these things mean. That castle, which I have spoken of above, is the Holy Church itself, which I built with my blood and that of my saints, and joined it with the cement of my charity, and placed in it my chosen ones and my friends.

13- The foundation of this is faith, that is, to believe that I am a just and merciful judge. But now the foundation is suffocated, because everyone believes in me and preaches mercy, but it seems that no one preaches and believes that I am a just judge.

14- They regard me as an unjust judge. For he would be an unjust judge who, out of mercy, would let the unjust go unpunished, so that the unjust might oppress the just all the more. But I am a just judge and merciful, so that I will not leave the least sin unpunished, nor the least good unrewarded.

15- Through the suffocation of this wall, those who sin without fear, who deny that I am righteous, and who disturb my friends in such a way as those who are in prison, enter the holy Church. For my friends have neither joy nor consolation, but all reproach and all pain are imposed on them as if they were demoniacs.

16- If they have told the truth about me, they are refuted and accused of lying. They are eager to hear or speak correctly, but there is no one to listen to them or speak correctly to them.

17- I too, God and creator, blaspheme. For they say: 'We do not know if there is a God. And if it is, we do not care.' My standard is prostrated and trampled upon, saying: 'Why did he suffer? What good is it to us? If he wants to give us our will, it is enough for us, and let him have his kingdom and heaven!' I also want to go to them, but they say: 'We will die before we leave our will.'

18- Behold, my bride, what they are! I did them and I could erase them with one word. How proud they are against me! But now, because of the prayers of my mother and of all the saints, I am still so merciful and patient, that I want to send them my words which have proceeded from my mouth and offer them my mercy.

19- If they are willing to receive it, I will appease them, but if not, they will feel my justice in such a way that like thieves they will be publicly confounded before angels and men and will be judged by all. For just as men hanged on a gallows are devoured by choirs, so these will be devoured by demons and not consumed.

20- Just as those who are punished in the wooden cage find no rest there, so these will have pain and bitterness on every side. A fiery river will flow into their mouths, and their bellies will not be filled, but they will be renewed from day to day to the punishment.

21- But my friends will be saved and will be comforted by the words that proceed from my mouth. They will see my justice with mercy. I will clothe them with the armor of my charity and make them so strong that the adversaries of the faith will fall back like mud and be forever ashamed when they see my justice, because they have abused my patience."

Chapter 6

Christ's words to the bride, how her spirit cannot be with the wicked, and about the separation of the bad from the good and about the sending of the good, armed with spiritual weapons, into war, that is, against the world.

1- My enemies are like the most ferocious beasts: they can never be satisfied or rest. Their heart is so empty of my love that the thought of my passion never enters it. Never once again did this word proceed from their innermost heart: 'Lord, you have redeemed us, praise be to you for your bitter passion!' How can my spirit be with those who have no divine love for me, who, in order to fulfill their will, willingly betray others?

2- Their hearts are full of the lowest worms, that is, the affections of the world. The devil has put his dung in their mouths, and therefore they do not like my words. Therefore, I will separate them from my friends with my sword. And just as there is no death more bitter than any death, so there is no punishment in which they do not share, and they will be cut in half by the devil and divided from me. They are so hateful to me, that I will say that all who adhere to them will be separated from me.

3- Therefore, I send my friends to separate the devils from my members, because they are truly my enemies. Therefore, I sent them as soldiers into the war. For everyone who afflicts his flesh and abstains from unlawful things is truly a soldier of mine.

4- They will have as spears my words that I have spoken with my mouth, a sword in their hand, that is, faith, in their breast will be the breastplate of charity, so that, whatever happens, they will love me no less. They must have a clip of patience at their side, that they may endure all things patiently. For I shut them up like gold in a jar, and now they must come out and walk in my way.

5- I could not have entered according to the justice ordered into the glory of majesty without tribulation with my humanity. How then shall they enter? If their Lord was reconciled, it is not surprising if they are also reconciled. If the Lord endured the blows, no great thing, if they themselves endure the words. Fear not, for I will never leave them. As it is impossible for the devil to touch and divide the heart of God, so it is impossible for the devil to separate them from me.

6- And because they are like the purest gold in my sight, therefore, if they are tried by a little fire, I will not leave them, but it is for their greater reward."

Chapter 7

Glorious words of the Virgin to her daughter about the manner of dressing and what should be the clothes and ornaments with which the daughter should be adorned and clothed.

1- I am Mary, who gave birth to the true God and the true man, the Son of God. I am the queen of the angels. My son loves you with all his heart. That's why you love him! You must be dressed in the most decent clothes. I will show you how and what they should be.

2- For just as you previously had a shirt, then a tunic, shoes, a cloak and a necklace on your chest, so you must have it spiritually now. The shirt is wrinkled. For as the shirt is nearer to the flesh, so contrition and confession is the first way of conversion to God. By this the mind, which rejoiced in sin, is cleansed, and the filthy flesh is restrained.

3- The two shoes are two affections, namely, the will to make amends and the will to do good and abstain from evil. Your tunic is your hope in God, because just as a tunic has two sleeves, so in hope there is justice and mercy, so that you hope for the mercy of God, that you do not neglect his justice. And so think of his justice and judgment, so that you do not forget his mercy, because he does not do any justice without mercy, nor mercy without justice.

4- Faith is a cloak. For as the cloak covers all things and all things are contained in it, so by faith a man can comprehend and reach all things. This mantle must be sprinkled with signs of the love of your spouse, namely how he created you, how he redeemed you, how he nourished you and brought you into his spirit and opened your spiritual eyes.

5- The necklace is a reflection of his passion. May this always be fixed on your chest, how he was mocked and scourged, how he stood alive on the cross bleeding and with all his nerves pierced, how in death his whole body trembled from the passion of the most acute pain, how he commended his spirit into the hands of his father. May this necklace always be on your chest.

6- Let there be a crown on your head, that is, chastity in your affections, so that you would rather suffer blows than be defiled any more. Then be shy and honest. Think of nothing, desire nothing but your God, your Creator, whom you have, you have everything. And so, you will wait for your bridegroom to get dressed."

Chapter 8

The words of the queen of heaven to her beloved daughter, informing her how the Son should love and praise her together with her mother.

1- I am the queen of heaven. You are worried about how you should praise me. Know for certain that all the praise of my son is my praise. And he who dishonors him dishonors me, because I loved him so fervently and he loved me, that we were as it were one heart. And he himself honored me, who was an earthly vessel, so honorably that he exalted me above all the angels.

2- Therefore, you must praise me: 'Blessed are you, God, creator of all things, who deigned to descend into the womb of the virgin Mary. Blessed are you, O God, who willed to be with the virgin Mary without reproach, and from her you deigned to take immaculate flesh without sin. Blessed are you, O God, who came to the virgin with the joy of her soul and of all her members, and with the joy of all her members went forth from her without sin.

3- Blessed are you, God, who comforted the virgin Mary, your mother, after your ascension with frequent consolations and visited her by yourself consoling her. Blessed are you, O God, who took the body and soul of the virgin Mary, your mother, into heaven and placed them in honor above all the angels next to your divinity. Pity me because of his prayers!'"

Chapter 9

Words to the queen of heaven to the beloved concerning the sweetest love which the Son had for the virgin mother, and how the mother of Christ was conceived from a chaste marriage and sanctified in the womb, and how she was taken up in body and soul into heaven, and about the virtues of her name and good and bad angels, assigned to men.

1- I am the queen of heaven. Love my son, because he is most honest, and when you have him, you have all honesty. He is also the most desirable, and when you have him, you have everything desirable. Love him, because he is the most virtuous, and when you have him, you have all the virtues.

2- I want to tell you how sweetly he loved my body, how sweetly my soul, how much he even honored my name. My son himself loved me before I loved him, because he is my creator. He joined the marriage of my father and mother with such chastity, that at that time no more chaste couple could be found, and they would never marry except according to the law, only for the purpose of raising a child.

3- And when it was announced to them by an angel that they would give birth to a virgin, from which the salvation of the world would proceed, they would rather die than meet with carnal love, and pleasure was dead in them. However, I tell you for certain that out of divine love and from the word of the announcing angel they came together in the flesh, not out of concupiscence of any pleasure but against their will out of divine love, and thus my flesh was united from their seed through divine love.

4- And when my body was made, God sent the soul created by his divinity into the body, and soon the soul was sanctified with the body, which the angels guarded and guarded day and night. But when the soul was sanctified and joined to the body, so much happiness came to my mother that it was impossible to say. Then, in the full course of my life, first my soul, because it was the mistress of the body, it lifted up to divinity more excellent than the rest, and then my body, so that no creature's body is so near to God as mine.

5- Behold, how much my son loved my soul and my body! But there are some who, with an evil spirit, deny that I have been taken up body and soul; some, indeed, who do not know better. But this is the most certain truth of the matter, that I was taken up with body and soul to divinity.

6- My son has honored my name, listen! My name is Mary, as it is read in the Gospel. When the angels hear this name, they rejoice in their consciousness and give thanks to God, who has done such grace through me and with me, and that they see the humanity of my son glorified in the deity.

7- Those who are in purgatory rejoice beyond measure, as if he were lying in bed, if he hears from some a word of comfort and that which pleases him in his heart, which immediately exults.

8- The angels also, on hearing this name of good, immediately draw nearer to the righteous, whom they have been given to guard, and rejoice at their departure, because good angels are given to all men for guarding, and evil angels for trial. It is not so that the angels themselves are separated from God, but they guard the soul in such a way that they do not leave God but are constantly in his presence and yet inflame and incite the soul to do good.

9- Even the demons fear this name and fear it. Those who, hearing this name Mary, immediately leave their souls from the claws with which they held it. For just as a fowl, which has its claws and beak on its prey, if it hears any sound, leaves the prey, and when it sees nothing to do, it immediately returns to the same, so the demons, on hearing my name, immediately leave their souls as if terrified, but again they cry out and return to it. like a very swift arrow, unless some amendment follows.

10- Indeed, no one is so cold from the love of God, unless he is condemned, if he invokes this name with this intention, that he never wants to return to his usual work, that the devil does not depart from him at once, and never again returns to him, unless he resumes his will to sin mortally. However, sometimes it is permitted for him to disturb him for the sake of his greater reward, but not to possess it.

Chapter 10

The words of the virgin Mary to her daughter, useful teaching, how she should live, presentation and many wonderful declarations of Christ's passion.

1- I am the queen of heaven, the mother of God. I told you that you should have a necklace on your chest. Now I will show you more fully, that from the beginning, when I heard and understood that there was a God, I was always anxious and fearful about my safety and obedience. But when I had heard more fully that God himself was my creator and judge of all my actions, I loved him deeply, and every hour I feared and thought lest I should offend him by word or deed.

2- Then when I had heard that he had given the law to the people and his precepts and had done so many wonderful things with them, I decided firmly in my heart to love nothing but him, and the worldly things were intensely bitter to me. After hearing this, that the same God was going to redeem the world and be born of a virgin, I was moved with such love for him that I thought of nothing but God, I wanted nothing but him.

3- I distanced myself, as much as I could, from the conversations and presence of my parents and friends, and I gave all that I could have to those in need. I spared nothing but thin food and clothing. None but God pleased me. I always wished in my heart that I might live to the time of his birth, if by chance I might deserve to become an unworthy handmaid of the mother of God. I vowed in my heart, if it were acceptable to him, to observe my virginity, and never to possess anything in the world.

4- But if God willed otherwise, His will would be done, not mine, because I believed that He could do all things and willed nothing but what was good for me. Therefore, I committed all my will to him.

5- But at the instant when the virgins were presented in the temple of the Lord according to the constitution, I was also among them because of the obedience of my parents, thinking with myself that nothing is impossible to God. And since he himself knew that I longed for nothing, wanted nothing but himself, he could keep me in my virginity, if it pleased him; but if it were, his will would be done.

6- And having heard all that was commanded in the temple, I returned home to a greater extent than before. For this reason I distanced myself more than usual from all, and was alone nights and days, fearing most vehemently lest my mouth should speak, or my ears should hear anything against my God, or my eyes should see anything pleasing. I was also timid in silence, and much anxious, lest I should perhaps have kept silent when I ought to have spoken more.

7- And when I was thus troubled in my heart, alone with myself, and entrusting all my hope to God, immediately it came into my mind to think of the great power of God, how the angels and all created things serve him, what is his glory, which is ineffable and endless.

8- And when I was wondering about this, I saw three wonderful things. For I saw a star, but not such as shines from heaven. I saw a light, but not such as shines in the world. I felt a smell, but not of the quality of herbs or anything like that, but very sweet and truly indescribable, with which I was completely filled and exalted with joy. Then immediately I heard a voice, but not from a human mouth. And when I heard them, I was quite afraid, considering that it might not be an illusion.

9- And immediately an angel of God appeared before me as a most beautiful man, but not clothed with flesh, who said to me: 'Alas, full of grace!' etc. When I heard this, I wondered what this meant, or why he uttered such a greeting. For I knew myself and believed that I was unworthy of such a thing or of any good thing, yet it was not impossible for God to do whatever He willed.

10- Then the angel said a second time: 'That which shall be born in thee is holy, and shall be called the Son of God, and as it pleaseth him, so shall it be.' And yet I did not believe that I was worthy, nor did the angel ask: 'Why' or 'When will it be?' And the angel answered me, as I said, that nothing is impossible to God, but that whatever He wills to do, it will be done, etc.

11- When I heard the word of the angel, I had the most fervent feeling that I was the mother of God, and my soul spoke out of love: 'Here I am, let your will be done in me!' At which word my son was immediately conceived in my womb with inexpressible exultation of my soul and of all my members.

12- And when I had him in the womb, I carried him without pain, without heaviness and weariness of the belly. I humbled myself in all things, knowing that he was almighty whom I bore. But when I gave birth to him, I gave birth to him without pain and sin, just as I had conceived, with such exultation of soul and body, that my feet did not feel the ground where they stood before exultation. And just as my soul entered with joy into all my members, so with the joy of all my members the exulting soul went out with unspeakable joy without injury to my virginity.

13- And when I beheld and considered his beauty, my soul dropped like dew for joy, knowing that I was unworthy of such a son. But when I considered the places of the nails in the hands and feet of those whom I had heard to be crucified according to the prophets, then my eyes were filled with tears, and my heart seemed to be rent with sorrow. And then my son looked at me with tears in his eyes and was sad as if to death.

14- But when I considered the power of his deity, I was comforted again, knowing that he would so will and so arrange, and I conformed all my will to his will. And so, my joy was always mingled with sorrow.

15- At the moment of my son's passion, his enemies seized him, struck him on the cheek and neck, and spitting on him, mocked him. Then being led to the pillar, he personally stripped himself of his clothes and personally applied his hands to the pillar, which the enemies had bound mercilessly.

16- But the bound man had no covering at all, but, as he was born, he stood thus and accepted the embarrassment of his nakedness. But his enemies rose up, who, fleeing from their friends, hounded and scourged his body, cleansed from all stain and sin.

17- At the first blow I, who stood nearer, fell as if dead, and with renewed breath I saw his body beaten and scourged up to his ribs, so that his ribs were visible. And what was more bitter, when the whips were withdrawn, his flesh was furrowed with the whips.

18- And when my son was standing all bleeding, all so torn, that no health could be found in him, nor could anything be scourged, then one of them, in an excited spirit, asked: 'Will you kill him thus unjustly?' And immediately followed his chains.

19- Then my son put on his own clothes. Then I saw the place where my son's feet had stood completely filled with blood, and I recognized his footsteps from my son's footsteps. For as he proceeded, it appeared that the ground was infused with blood.

20- They did not agree that he should put on his clothes, but pushed and dragged him to haste. But when he was led away as a thief, my son himself wiped the blood from his eyes. And when he had been judged, they laid upon him a cross to bear. And when she had carried it a little, one coming took it upon himself to carry it.

21- Meanwhile, when my son was going to the place of passion, some struck him on the neck, others on the face. And he was smitten so strongly and powerfully that, although I did not see him smiting, I heard clearly the sound of the smiting. And when I had come with him to the place of his passion, I saw all the instruments prepared there for his death. And my son himself, coming there, stripped himself personally of his clothes, the officers saying among themselves: 'These are our clothes, and he will not take them back, because he has been condemned to death.'

22- And when my son was standing, as he was born, with his body naked, one then ran and brought him a veil, with which he himself, rejoicing, hid his private parts. Afterwards the torturers seized him and laid him on the cross, first fixing his right hand to the stake, which had been pierced for nails. And they pierced the hand itself from that part where the mouth was stronger. Then, drawing his other hand with a rope, they fastened it to the stake in a similar manner.

23- Then they crucified the right foot, and over the left one with two nails, so that all the tendons and veins were stretched out and broken. When this was done, they fitted a crown of thorns to his head, which stung my son's head so violently that his eyes were filled with flowing blood, his ears were blocked, and his beard was disfigured with the blood that flowed down. And when he stood thus bleeding and pierced, sympathizing with me standing and groaning, he looked with bloodshot eyes at John, my sister, and commended me to him.

24- At that time I heard others saying that my son was a thief, others that he was a liar, others that no one was more worthy of death than my son. At the hearing of which my pain was renewed. But, as has been said, when the first nail was driven into it, at the first blow I fell down as if dead, my eyes darkened, my hands trembling, my feet shaking. And I did not look back with bitterness, until it was completely attached.

25- But when I got up I saw my son hanging miserably, and I, his mother most distressed, terrified on every side, could scarcely stand before the pain. But my son, seeing me and his friends weeping inconsolably, cried out with a mournful and loud voice to his Father, saying: 'Father, why have you forsaken me?' as if he were saying: 'There is no one who will have mercy on me but you, Father.'

26- Then his eyes appeared half-dead, his jaw sunken and his countenance mournful, his mouth open and his tongue bloody, his belly stuck to his back with consumed moisture, as if he had no entrails, his whole-body pale and languid from the flow and egress of blood. His hands and feet were stretched out rigidly and were drawn and shaped in the form of a cross. His beard and hair were all sprinkled with blood.

27- And so, when my son stood thus torn and livid, only his heart was fresh, because he was of the best and strongest nature. For out of my flesh, he took the cleanest and best-complexioned body.

28- His skin was so tender and thin that he was never whipped so lightly without blood immediately coming out. His blood, too, was so fresh that it could be seen on his clean skin. And because he was in the best of nature, life struggled with death in his pierced body.

29- For sometimes the pain from the pierced limbs and nerves of the body ascended to the heart, which was very fresh and uncorrupted, and tormented him with incredible pain and suffering. And sometimes pain descended from the heart into the torn limbs, and thus prolonged death with bitterness.

30- And when my son, surrounded by these pains, looked at his weeping friends, who would rather have suffered that pain in themselves with his help, or to burn eternally in hell than to see him thus tortured, that pain from the pain of his friends, all the bitterness and tribulation, either in body or He endured in his heart, he left, because he loved to hold them. Then, from the extreme distress of the body, on the part of humanity, he cried out to the Father: 'O Father, into your hands I commend my spirit.'

31- Therefore, when I, his most devoted mother, heard this voice, all my limbs trembled with the bitter pain of my heart. And every time afterwards I thought of this voice, as if it were present and fresh in my ear. And when death drew nigh, when the heart was broken by the violence of the pains, then all his limbs trembled, and his head bowed as if raising himself a little, his mouth seemed to be open, and his tongue all bloody.

32- His hands withdrew themselves a little from the place of the perforation and supported the weight of the body on his feet. The fingers and arms stretched out in a certain way, and the back was strongly braced against the log.

33- Then some said to me: 'Mary, your son is dead.' But others said: 'He is dead, but he will rise again.' So when they all departed, one coming up stuck a lance in his side with such force that it almost passed through his other side. And when the spear was drawn out, the tip appeared red with blood. Then it seemed to me that my heart was pierced, when I saw the heart of my dearest son pierced.

34- Then he was taken down from the cross. I received him on my knee as if he were a leper and all livid. For his eyes were dead and full of blood, his mouth was cold as snow, his beard was like a reed, his face was contracted. They had also directed their hands in such a way that they could not be put down except around the navel. As he stood on the cross, I had him on my knees like a man contracted in all his limbs.

35- Afterwards they laid him in a linen cloth, and with my linen I wiped out his wounds and limbs, and closed his eyes and mouth, which had been open in death.

36- Then they put him in the tomb. Oh, how gladly would I have been married to my son then, if it had been his will!

37- When these were completed, that good John came and led me into the house. Behold, my daughter, my son endured such things for you!"

Chapter 11

Christ's words to his bride, how he gave himself up voluntarily to his crucifixion of enemies, and about the way of living in the continence of all members from illicit movements, as the example of his most sweet passion.

1- The Son of God spoke to the bride, saying: "I am the creator of heaven and earth, and my body is true, which is consecrated on the altar. Love me with all your heart, because I loved you and I voluntarily gave myself up to my enemies, and my friends and my mother remained in bitter pain and weeping.

2- And when I saw the lance, the nails, the whips, and other kinds of suffering prepared, I proceeded without any means to the passion. And when my head was covered with blood on every side, and the blood flowed from every side, and if my enemies had still touched my heart, I would rather suffer this to be broken and wounded than to be without you.

3- Therefore, you are very ungrateful if you do not love me for such love. For if my head is the point and bowed on the cross for you, your head must be bowed in humility. And because my eyes were bloodshot and full of tears, therefore your eyes must refrain from the pleasant sight. And because my ears were filled with blood and heard the words of my reproach, therefore your ears are turned away from scurrilous and foolish expressions.

4- Because indeed my mouth has been drunk with the bitterest drink and forbidden from good things, therefore let your mouth be stopped from evils and opened to good things. And because my hands are extended with nails, therefore your works, which are shaped in your hands, should be extended to the poor and to my commandments.

5- Your feet, that is, your affections, with which you must go to me, be crucified by pleasures, so that, just as I have suffered in all my members, so all your members may be prepared for my obedience. Because I demand a greater service from you than from others, because I have done you a greater favor."

Chapter 12

How the angel asks for the bride and how Christ complains of the angel, what is it that he complains for the bride, and what is expedient for the bridegroom.

1- The good angel, the guardian of the bridegroom, seemed to beg Christ for the same bride. To whom the Lord answered, saying: "He who wishes to pray for another must pray for his salvation. For you are like a fire that is never extinguished, burning unceasingly with my love. You see and know everything when you see me. You want nothing but what I am." Tell me, then, what is good for my new bride!"

2- And he answered: "Lord, you know everything." To whom the Lord said: "Indeed, everything, whatever has been and will be, is eternally in me, and everything in heaven and on earth I know and know and there is no change with me, however, so that this bride may understand my will, tell her only to the listener, what It's good for him!"

3- And the angel said: "He has a lofty heart and a great heart. That is why a rod is necessary for him to tame." And then the Lord said: "What then do you ask of him, my friend?" And he: "Lord, I ask for mercy with your rod." And the Lord said: "Because of you I will do this to him, who never do justice without mercy. Therefore, this bride must love me with all her heart."

Chapter 13

How the enemy of God has three demons in him and about the judgment brought against him by Christ.

1- My enemy has three demons in him. The first sits in the genitals, the second in the heart, the third in the mouth. The first is like a sailor who causes water to enter through the keel, which gradually increases and fills the ship. Then the water overflows and the ships are submerged.

2- This is the sailors' body, driven by the temptations of demons and their lusts like storms, into which their pleasure first entered through the hull, that is, the pleasure with which they delighted in such thoughts. And because he did not resist through penance, nor did he strengthen himself by abstinence, he increased every day by using the water of pleasure in consent. Then the concupiscence of the ship's belly having been completed or filled, the water flowed out and covered the ship with pleasure, so that it would not come to the port of salvation.

3- The second demon, which sits in the heart, is like a worm lying in an apple, which first eats the core of the apple, and then, leaving its dung there, spreads throughout the whole apple until it becomes completely empty. That's what the devil does. First, let him conquer his will and his good desires, which are like a nucleus, from which all strength of mind and good subsist, and having emptied his heart of these goods, he then leaves in his heart the thoughts and affections of the world for them, as if he loved them more.

4- Now he pushes the very body to what he likes, and from this his strength and intelligence are diminished and he grows weary of life. He is most certainly an apple without a core, that is, a man without a heart, because he enters my Church without a heart, because he has no divine charity.

5- The third demon is like an archer who, looking through the windows, shoots at the unsuspecting. How does a demon sit in him who never speaks without him? For that which is more loved, is more frequently mentioned. His bitter words, with which he wounds others, are like arrows that are shot through so many windows, whenever the devil is mentioned, whenever the innocent are wounded by his words, whenever the simple are offended by his words.

6- Therefore, in my truth, who am the truth, I swear that I will judge him as a harlot to the brimstone fire, as a traitor and a traitor to the cutting of all his limbs and as a despiser of his Lord to perpetual confusion. However, as long as soul and body are at the same time, my mercy is open to him.

7- Now this is what I require of him, namely, that he attend more frequently to the divine, that he fears no reproach and covets no honor, and that he never mentions an evil name in his mouth."

8- Here he buried the excommunicated prior of the Cistercian order. And when he had read the last commendation for him, the lady heard in spirit: "He did as he could and buried him.

9- Now know for certain that he will be the first to be buried after this dead man. For he sinned against the Father, who said that he is not an acceptor of persons, nor honors the countenance of a long time against justice. But here, for the sake of a little corruption, he honored the unworthy, and placed him, as he ought not, among the worthy.

10- He also sinned against my Spirit, which is the fellowship and fellowship of the righteous, when he buried the unjust with the righteous. He also sinned against me, the Son, because I said: 'He who rejects me will be rejected.' But he honored him and exalted him, whom my church and my vicar despised."

Chapter 14

Christ's words to the bride about the manner and respect that she should hold in prayer, and about the three kinds of people in this world who serve God.

1- I am your God, who, crucified on the cross, true God and true man in one person, I am every day in the hands of the priest. When you make any prayer to me, always conclude your prayer in this way, so that you wish always to be my will, not yours. Because when you plead for the damned, I do not hear you.

2- And sometimes I will do what you wish against your salvation, and therefore it is necessary for you to commit your will to me, who knows all things, who provides you with nothing but good. For many do not pray with the right intention, and therefore do not deserve to be heard.

3- For there are three kinds of men who serve me in this world. They are the first who believe that I am God and giver of all and powerful over all. These men serve me with this intention, that they may desire temporal things and honor, but heavenly things are nothing to them, and they gladly lose them, that they may desire presence. To these according to their will comes the prosperity of the age in all things. And thus having lost the eternal ones, I repay them in temporal convenience, whatever good they have done for me, to the last quarter and to the very last point.

4- The second are those who believe that I am an omnipotent God and a strict judge, and those close to me almost out of fear, but not out of love for heavenly glory. For unless they were afraid, they would not serve me.

5- There are third parties who believe that I am the creator of all and the true God, who believe that I am just and merciful. And they open their doors to me not out of fear of anyone, but out of divine love and love. And indeed they would rather bear all the punishment, if it were sufficient, than to provoke me once to anger. But they deserve to be heard in their prayer, because their will is according to my will.

6- For the first shall never come out of the punishment nor see my face. But the second will not have such a great punishment, nor will he see my face, unless he corrects that fear by penance.

Chapter 15

Christ's words to the bride, the appropriating conditions of the great king to Christ, and of the two gazophilacies, by which the love of God and the love of the world are signified, and of the doctrine of progressing in this life.

1- I am like one great and mighty king. For there are four things that belong to a king: first, he must be pious, second, meek, third, wise, and fourth, charitable. I am truly the king of angels and of all men. I also have those four properties that I mentioned.

2- For in the first place I am the richest, because I give all what is necessary, and I have no less after what has been given. Secondly, I am very gentle, because I am ready to give to all who ask. Thirdly, therefore, I am the wisest, because I know what is due and expedient to each one. Fourthly, I am more charitable, because I am more ready to give than someone to ask.

3- I have like two gazophilacia. For in the first gazophilacus there are stores as heavy and heavy as lead, and that room where they are is surrounded by sharp stinging thorns. But he who first begins to turn and reroll them, and then learns to carry them, will afterwards seem to him as light as a feather. And so they become very light, which before seemed heavy, and soft, which were thought to sting before.

4- In the second chamber there appears to be glittering gold and precious stones and fragrant cups and sweetmeats. But really that gold is yellow, and those cups are poisonous.

5- For there are two ways to this gazophilacia, but before there was only one way. At the crossroads, that is, at the entrance of two roads, a man stood and cried out to three men who were walking by another road, saying: 'Listen, listen to my words, and if you will not hear, at least see with your own eyes, for what I speak is true. But if you will not hear or see, at least shake your hands and prove that there is no falsehood in my words.'

6- Then the first of them said: 'Let us hear and see if his words are true.' The second man says: 'Whatever he says is false.' A third said: 'I know that what he says is true, but I do not care.'

7- What are these two passions but my love and the love of the world? But to this there are two gazophilias in two ways: I reject and completely deny the proper will, which leads to my love, and the pleasure of the flesh, which leads to the love of the world.

8- But in my love it seems to some that there is a burden like lead, because when they must fast and watch or restrain the flesh, they seem to carry it as if they were lead. But if they have heard words and insults, if they linger in religion and prayer, they dwell as if they were among thorns, and are distressed at every hour.

9- But whoever wants to be in my love, let him first begin to turn the burden, that is, he should try to do good things through will and continuous desire. Then he eases up little by little, that is, he does what he can, thinking thus: 'I can do this well, if God gives me help.'

10- Then, continuing in the enterprise with such enthusiasm, he begins to bear those things which seemed to him to be burdensome before, so that all labor in fasting or vigils and other labors of any kind is as light as a feather to him. And my friends rest in such a seat, which is to the wicked and treacherous as if surrounded by thorns and thistles, but to my friends it is as calm and gentle as a rose.

11- To this gazophilicium the right way is the contempt properly of the will, when a man, considering my passion and love, does not care to do his will and resists with all his strength and always strives for greater things.

12- And although this road is somewhat steep in the beginning, yet in the process it gives much pleasure, to the extent that those things which at first seemed impossible to bear, afterwards become very easy, so that he may rightly say within himself: 'The yoke of God is easy.'

13- According to the gazophilacium is the world in which there are gold, precious stones, and cups, which seem fragrant, but when tasted are bitter like poison. For every one who carries gold, it happens to him that, when his body is weakened and his limbs fail, and when his marrow is annihilated and his body falls through death to the earth, then he leaves the gold and the stones, and they are of no more value to him than clay.

14- Even the cups of the world, that is, pleasures, seem delightful, but when they come into the belly, they weaken the head, weigh down the heart and make all the members fall, and afterwards a man dries up like hay. And when the pain of death approaches, everything pleasant becomes bitter like poison.

15- To this gazophilia leads one's own will, when a man does not care to resist his right affections, nor does he meditate, which I commanded and did, but whatever comes into his thinking, whether lawful or unlawful, he immediately does.

16- On this road walk three men, by whom I mean all the reprobates, who love the world and all their own will. To these I cried, who stood at the gates or at the entrance of the ways, because coming in human flesh I showed men two ways, namely, what should be followed and what should be avoided, namely, which way led to life and which to death. For before my coming in the flesh there was but one way, by which all the good and the bad went to hell.

17- But I am the one who cried out, and I cried out like this: 'O people, listen to my words, which lead to the way of life, because they are true, and you can perceive with your own sense that these are the truths that I speak. And if you do not hear them or cannot hear them, at least see them, that is, with faith and understanding, because my words are true. For as with the eyes of the flesh something visible is seen, so with the eyes of faith invisible things can be seen and believed.

18- Finally, there are many simple people in the Church, who do a few good things, yet are saved by faith, by which they believe that I am the creator and redeemer of all. For there is no one who cannot understand that I am God and believe, if he considers, how the earth produces fruit and how the sky gives rain, how the trees grow, how the animals subsist each in its own kind, how the stars sow to man, how the opposites of man's will come to pass.

19- From all these a man can see that he is mortal, and that God is the one who arranges all these things. For if there were no God, all these things would go on in disorder. Therefore, all things are from God and all things are rationally arranged for the edification of man. There is not the least thing in the world that exists or exists without reason. Therefore, if a man cannot, because of weakness, grasp or understand my power as it is, he can still see by faith and believe.

20- And if, O men, you refuse to consider my power with your understanding, you can still draw with your hands the works which I and my saints have done. Because they are so open that no one can doubt that they are the works of God.

21- Who raised the dead and enlightened the blind but God? Who cast out the demons but God? But what did I teach but useful things for the health of soul and body and light things to carry?' But the first man says, that is, some say: 'Let us hear and prove whether they are true!' These stand for a time in my service, not for the sake of choice, but for the experience and imitation of others, neither abandoning their own will, but doing theirs with my will.

22- These are in a dangerous position, because they want to serve two masters, although they can serve neither well. But when they have been called, they will be rewarded by the Lord whom they have loved more.

REVELATIONS

23- The second person says, that is, some: 'Whatever he speaks is false, and the Scripture is false.' I am God and the creator of all things, and without me nothing was made. I have established the new law and the old, and it has proceeded from my mouth, and there is no falsehood in it, because I am the truth. Therefore, those who say that I have spoken falsely and say that the Holy Scriptures are false, they themselves will never see my face, because their conscience tells them that I am God, because everything happens according to my will and my disposition.

24- The sky illuminates them, and they cannot illuminate themselves, the earth produces fruit, the air fertilizes the earth, all animals have a certain disposition, demons confess me, righteous people make incredible peace because of my love. They see all these things and yet do not see me.

25- Even they can see me in my justice, if they consider how the earth swallowed up the wicked, the fire burned up the unrighteous. Thus they can see me in my mercy, when water flowed from the rock to the righteous and the water of the sea yielded to them, when the fire did not hurt them, when the sky nourished them like the earth. And therefore because they see these things and still say that I lie, they will never see my face.

26- A third man says, that is, some: 'We know well that he is the true God, but we do not care.' They will be tormented forever, because they despise me, their God and Lord. Is it not a great contempt that they use my gifts, and yet they themselves disdain to serve me? For if they had it from their own energy and not entirely from me, it would be slight contempt.

27- But those who begin to turn my burden, that is, willingly and from fervent desire to try to do the little that they can, I will give grace to them. But those who lighten my burdens, that is to say, for my love, they prosper from day to day, I work with them, and I will be their strength and I will inflame them so that they want more.

28- But those who sit in a seat which seems to sting - yet it is very quiet - these are in labors and patience night and day and are not weary, but they burn all the more, and what they do seems to be a small matter to them. These are my dearest friends, and these are very few, because the cups of the second gazophila are more pleasing to others."

Chapter 16

How did the bridegroom look, because one of the saints spoke to God about a certain woman who had been terribly trampled on by a demon, who was later gloriously delivered by the prayers of the Virgin.

1- It seemed to the bridegroom that one of the saints was speaking to God, saying: "Why is the soul of this woman, whom you have redeemed with your blood, thus trampled by the devil?" The demon answered immediately, saying: "Because it is my right." And then the Lord said: "What is your right?" To which the demon answered: "There are two ways," he said. "One leads to heaven, the other to hell."

2- And when she looked both ways, she said to herself with her conscience and reason that she would rather choose my way. And because he had a free will to direct himself to whichever way he preferred, it seemed to him that it would be more useful to direct his will to the perpetration of sin, and then he began to walk along my path. Afterwards I deceived her with three vices, namely, gluttony, lust for money, and lust.

3- Therefore, I now sit in his womb and in his nature. And I held it with five hands. I hold his eyes with one hand so that he does not see spiritual things. With my second hand I hold his hand, lest he should do good works. With the third hand I hold his feet, lest he go to good things, and with the fourth hand I hold his understanding, lest he be ashamed of sinning. When I eat the fifth, I hold his heart with my hand, so that it does not return through contraction."

4- Then the blessed virgin Mary said to her son: "Son, compel him to tell the truth about the matter that I want to complain of him." And the son said: "You are my mother, you are the queen of heaven, you are the mother of mercy, you are the consolation of those who are in purgatory, you are the consolation of those who are wandering in the world. You are the lady of the angels; you are the most excellent with God. You are also the prince upon the devil. Preach thou, mother, these demons what thou wilt, and he will tell thee."

5- Then the Blessed Virgin asked that devil: "Tell me, devil, what intention did this woman have before she entered the Church?" To which the devil answered: "She herself had the will to abstain from sin." And the virgin Mary said to him: "Since the will which he had before was leading to hell, tell me, to what purpose does this will which he now only has, namely, to abstain from sin?" To which the devil replied: "The very will of abstinence leads itself to heaven." And then the virgin Mary said: "Because you received it from justice, that because of the previous will you led her from the way to the holy Church, now it is justice, that by that will she should be brought back to the Church."

6- And now I ask you, devil, further from you: Tell me, what kind of will does she have just at this point, in which her consciousness is now?" And the devil answered: "She herself has a contrition in her mind for these things she has done, and a great weeping, and He proposes never to commit such things any further but wishes to improve as much as he can."

7- Then the Virgin asked the devil: "Tell me, can these three sins, viz. lust, gluttony, and covetousness, with these three goods, viz., contrition, weeping, and the intention of amends, coexist in one heart?" To which the devil answered: "No."

8- And the blessed Virgin then said: "Tell me, then, which of these ought to flee from their heart and withdraw, are these three virtues, or perhaps those three vices, from which you say that they cannot dwell together in the same place?"

9- And the devil said: "I say that 'sins'." And then the Virgin answered: "Therefore the way to hell is closed to him, and the way to heaven is open to him." Then the Blessed Virgin further asked the devil: "Tell me, if a predator lies before the bridegroom's door, wanting to violate her, what will the bridegroom do then?"

10- The devil answered: "If that bridegroom is good and magnanimous, he must defend her and risk his life for hers." Then the Virgin said: "You are the worst of robbers, but the soul is the bride of the bridegroom, my son, who redeemed her with his own blood. Therefore, you corrupted her and snatched her violently. Therefore, because my son is the bridegroom of the soul and is lord over you, therefore it is right for you to flee before him."

11- This same harlot wanted to return to the century, because the devil tormented her day and night to such an extent that he visibly lowered her eyes and dragged her out of bed in front of many people. Then, to the many faithful present, the lady St. Bridget said plainly:

12- "Go away, devil, because you have disturbed this creature of God enough." And when the word had been said, the woman lowered her eyes to the ground for half an hour and said, "Truly, I saw the devil in the most vile form coming out of the window, and I heard a voice saying to me: 'Truly, woman, you are delivered.'"

13- And after that hour the same woman was freed from all impatience and did not put up with dirty thoughts any longer, and she rested with a good end.

Chapter 17

Christ's words to the bride, how the sinner is likened to the tribe, that is, the eagle, the fowler and the boxer.

1- I am Jesus Christ, who is speaking to you, who in the womb of a virgin was true God and true man, no less ruling all things with the Father, although I was with a virgin. Such a worst enemy of mine is like a tribe: first, an eagle, flying in the air, under which other birds fly; secondly, he is like a bird singing in a pipe smeared with bitumen, whose voice the birds delight in, when they call to the pipe, are held back by that bitumen; the third is like a champion who is first in every contest.

2- For he is like an eagle, because through his pride, in which he would suffer no one, if he could, to be superior, he destroys all whom he can with his talons. Therefore, I will cut off his wings by his power and pride. I will take away his malice from the earth. But I will hand him over to the unquenchable pot, where he will be tormented without end, unless he amends himself.

3- He is also like a bird, because he attracts all to himself by the sweetness of his words and promises, but whoever comes to him is so caught in perdition that they can never escape from it. Therefore, the wings of hell will close his eyes, so that he may never see my glory but the eternal darkness of hell.

4- His ears are cut off, lest he hear the words of my mouth. From the sole of the foot to the top of the head they will make him bitter for sweetness, so that he may endure as many punishments as he has brought to destruction.

5- He is also like a boxer, who is the first in every malice to yield to no one and sets out to put everyone down. Therefore, as the boxer will be the first in every penalty, his penalty will always be renewed and will not fail. But as long as the soul is with the body, my mercy is ready for him."

6- This was a very powerful soldier, who greatly hated the clergy, imposing insulting words on them. Of which the previous and subsequent revelation was made.

7- The Son of God speaks: "O soldier of the world, complain to the wise, what happened to the proud Haman, who despised my people! Was it not a shameful death and a great confusion? Thus he will mock me and my friends.

8- Therefore, just as Israel did not mourn the death of Aman, neither do my friends mourn over his death, but he will die a most bitter death unless he amends himself." This is how it happened.

Chapter 18

Christ's words to the bride, how humility should be in the house of God and how religion is designated by such a house, and also that buildings and almsgiving, etc., should be made of the good acquired and the way to restore it.

1- In my house there must be humility, which is now completely despised. There must be a strong wall between men and women, for although I could defend all and keep all without a wall, yet because of the wiles and cunning of the devil I want one wall to divide both rooms, which is strong and not very high, but moderate.

2- Let the windows be very simple and bright, the roof moderately high, so that nothing appears there, except that which smells of humility. Because those who are now building houses for me are like the builders. To whom, when the master of the building enters, they receive him by the hair and rub him under their feet, they place clay in the loft and gold under their feet. They do the same to me.

3- For they build with clay, that is to say, they place these temporary shelters as if to heaven. But souls, which are more precious than gold, they do not care at all. If I want to approach them through my preachers or through good thoughts, they seize me by the hair and trample me under their feet, that is, they blaspheme me and regard my works and my words as contemptible as dirt. But they consider themselves much wiser. For if they wanted to build for me to my honor, they would build souls first.

4- But whoever builds my house, let him take great care that not a single penny comes to the building that has not been well and justly acquired. For there are many who know that they have ill-gotten goods, and yet do not grieve about this, nor have the will to restore and satisfy those who have been defrauded and robbed, although they could restore and satisfy if they wished. But still, because they think that they cannot possess them forever, they give to the churches a portion of those goods which they have unjustly acquired, as if by this donation they would appease me. But other goods, well acquired, they reserve for their posterity. I certainly don't like this.

5- For whoever would please me with his gifts, he should first have the affection to improve himself, and then do the good works that he could. He must also mourn and bewail the evils he has done, and then make restitution, if he can. And if he cannot, he must have the will to restore the defrauded.

6- Afterwards he must take care never to commit such things again. But if there were no survivors, to whom he should return the ill-gotten gains, then he could give them to me, who I can repay to all his own. And if it is not enough to repay, then, if he humbles himself to me with the intention of making amends and with a broken heart, I am ready to repay, and I can restore to all those who have been defrauded their parts, either in the present age or in the future.

7- I want to tell you what the house means that I want to build. For the house itself is religion, of which I myself am the foundation, who founded all things, and by whom all things were made and exist. In which house there are four walls.

8- The first is my justice, with which I will judge those who oppose this house. The second wall is my wisdom, with which I will enlighten the inhabitants with my knowledge and intelligence. The third is my power, by which I will strengthen them against the devices of the devil. The fourth wall is also my mercy, which welcomes all who ask for it.

9- In this wall is a gate of grace, through which all those who ask are received. The roof of the house is charity, with which I diligently cover my sins, lest they be judged for those sins. The window of the roof, through which the sun enters, is a reflection of my grace, through which the warmth of my divinity enters to the inhabitants.

10- But the fact that the wall must be strong and large means that no one is able to weaken my words or destroy them. But the fact that it must be moderately high means that my wisdom can be partially understood and understood, but never fully.

11- The simple and clear windows signify that although my words are simple, yet through them the light of divine knowledge will enter the world.

12- The moderately high roof means that my words will not be made manifest in an incomprehensible sense but in a comprehensible and intelligible sense."

Chapter 19

The words of the creator to the bride about the magnificence of his power, wisdom and virtue, and how those who are now called wise sin more against him.

1- I am the creator of heaven and earth. I have three with me. I am the most powerful, I am the wisest, I am also the most virtuous. For I am so powerful that the angels in heaven honor me, the demons in hell do not dare to look at me. All the elements are at my disposal.

2- I am also so wise that no one is able to trace my wisdom, so knowing that I know all that has been and all that is to come. I am also so reasonable that not even the smallest thing, whether a worm or any other animal, however deformed it may be, is made without a cause.

3- I am also so virtuous that all good things flow from me as from a good fountain, and as from a vine all goodness proceeds with sweetness. Therefore no one can be powerful without me, wise without me, virtuous without me. And therefore, the very mighty of the ages sin against me, to whom I gave strength and power, that they might honor me, but they themselves ascribe honor to themselves, as if they had it from themselves.

4- The poor do not consider their weakness. For if I were to give them the slightest weakness, they would immediately fail and everything would be worthless to them. But how then could they withstand my strength and eternal punishments?

5- But those who are now called wise sin more against me. For I gave them sense and understanding and wisdom, that they might love me, but they understand nothing but their own temporal benefit. They have eyes in the back of their head, they see to their pleasures, but they have fallen to doing gracias to me, who gave them everything, because, whether good or bad, no one could feel and understand without me, although I allow evil to bend their will to what they want.

6- No one can be virtuous without me. Therefore, I can now say this proverb, which is commonly said by the common people: 'He who is patient is despised by all.' Thus I, because of my patience, seem too foolish to all, and therefore I am despised by all.

7- But woe to them, when I will show them my judgment after such patience! For they will be like clay before me, which falls into the abyss and does not stop until it reaches the depths of hell."

Chapter 20

The welcome conversation of the virgin Mother and Son, and the virgin Mother and Son to the bride, and how the bride should prepare herself for the wedding.

1- The mother seemed to say to her son: "Glory be to you, my son, you are the king over all lords, you created the heavens and the earth and all that is in them. Let all your desire be done, all your will be done!"

2- The son answered: "There is an old proverb that 'that which a youth learns in his youth, this he retains in his old age.' Thus you, mother, learned from your youth to follow my will and to leave all your will for me. That is why you well said: 'Thy will be done!'

3- For you are like precious gold, which is stretched out and beaten on a hard anvil, because you were beaten by all tribulations and in my passion you were reconciled before others, because when my heart was broken on the cross by the vehemence of pain, your heart was wounded by this as if by a very sharp sword, and you would gladly have allowed it to be divided, if it had been my will.

4- But I will say that if you could have resisted my passion and wished for my life, you did not want it except according to my will. That is why you said well: 'Thy will be done!'

5- Then Mary spoke to the bride: "Bride of my son, love my son, because he loves you! Honor his saints who stand by him! For they are like innumerable stars, who's light and splendor cannot be compared to any temporal light, because they are like the light of the world differs from darkness, so much more does the light of the saints differ from the light of this world.

6- I tell you truly, that if the saints were seen in their brightness, as they are, no human eye could bear this, but it would be deprived of bodily light."

7- Then the son of the Virgin spoke to his bride, saying: "My bride, you must have four. First, you must be prepared for the nuptials of my deity, in which there is no carnal lust, but a spiritual pleasure of the most gentle kind, such as it is fitting to have God with a chaste soul, so that not the love of your children, not even those of your parents or of your parents, may draw you back from my love. May it not happen to you like those foolish virgins who were unprepared when the Lord wanted to call them to marriage and were therefore excluded.

8- Secondly, you must be credulous with my words. For I am the truth, and nothing but the truth ever proceeds from my mouth, and no one can find in my words anything but the truth. Because sometimes I spiritually understand what I am speaking, sometimes as then the letter itself sounds, and my very words must then be understood nakedly, and therefore no one can accuse me of lying.

9- Thirdly, you must be obedient, so that there is no member in which you have sinned, from whom you do not demand a worthy penance and correction. For though I am merciful, I do not forsake justice. Therefore, to those to whom you are bound, obey humbly and cheerfully, so that I may do what seems useful and reasonable to you, and do not do contrary to obedience. For it is better for the sake of obedience to leave your will, even if it is good, and to follow the will of the commanding one, if it is not contrary to the salvation of the soul or otherwise unreasonable.

10- Fourthly, you must be humble, because you are joined to a spiritual marriage. Therefore, you must be humble and shy at the approach of your spouse. Let your handmaid be controlled and restrained, that is, your body restrained and well disciplined. For you will be a fruitful spiritual seed that will benefit many. For just as, if a shoot is inserted into a dry trunk, the trunk begins to blossom, so you must bear fruit and blossom with my grace, which will also intoxicate you, so that all the heavenly host may rejoice from the sweet wine that I am about to give you.

11- Do not distrust my goodness! I tell you for certain that just as Zacharias and Elizabeth rejoiced inwardly with indescribable joy at the promise of a future child, so you too will rejoice at my grace, which I want to do for you, and moreover others will rejoice through you.

12- An angel spoke to those two, namely Zacharias and Elizabeth, but I, God and creator of angels and your God, speak with you. These two have begotten me my dearest friend John, and through you I want to beget many children for me, not carnal but spiritual.

13- I tell you truly, that John himself was like a reed full of sweetness and honey, because nothing unclean ever entered his mouth, nor did he take more than the perceptible measure necessary for life. "Never did a seedier humor come out of his body, and therefore he may well be called an angel and a virgin."

Chapter 21

The words of the bridegroom to the bride in the best figure of a certain magician, by whom the devil is wonderfully depicted and explained.

1- Jesus, the bridegroom, spoke to his bride in the figure of a frog, saying: "A certain magician had the best and most brilliant gold. A simple and meek man came to him and wanted to buy that gold. To whom the magician said: 'You will not have this gold, but better gold and you will give me a greater quantity.'

2- To whom he said: 'I,' said he, 'so much desire to have that gold of yours, that I, before I lose it, will give it to you, as you wish.' And when the magician had given him better and greater gold, he took from him the bright gold and put it in the chest, thinking of making a ring for himself on his finger.

3- And after a little intermission, the magician came to that simple man, saying: 'This gold which you have bought and placed in your chest, is not gold, as you think, but a very cheap frog, which was nourished in my breast and fed on my food. And to prove that this is true, open the cupboard, and you will see that a frog will jump into my breast, on which it was nourished.'

4- And when he was about to open it and try it, a frog appeared in the chest, the lid of which hung on four hinges, as if a frog had fallen. Then, when the door of the chest was opened, the frog, seeing the magician, jumped into his chest. Seeing that the nobles and the friends of that simple man said to him: 'Sir', they say, 'that best gold lies in the frog, and if you wanted, you could easily obtain the gold.'

5- And he: 'How', he said, 'how could I do this?' They said: 'If someone were to take a very sharp and fierce spear and thrust it into the frog's back, and from that part of the back where there was something hollow, then he would be able to obtain gold more quickly. But if a hollow could not be found in it, then the lance must have been driven into it very strongly and with all the effort, and thus you could have what you bought.'

6- Who is this magician but the devil, who suggests to men pleasures and honors which are nothing but vain. For he promises falsities to be true and makes truths seem false. For he owns that precious gold, that is, the soul, which I made more precious than all the stars and planets by the power of my deity, which I created immortal and stable and more delightful than the rest, and I prepared for him with myself an eternal rest and habitation.

7- This I bought from the power of the devil with better gold and a greater price, when I gave my flesh for her, free from all sin, and endured such bitter suffering that not a member of mine was without a wound. And the soul having been redeemed, I placed it in the body as in a chest, until I placed it in the dignity of my deity.

8- But now the soul of man thus redeemed has become like the vilest and most vile frog, dancing through pride and dwelling at dinner through lust, and has taken away from me my gold, that is, all my righteousness. And therefore, the devil may well say to me: 'The gold which you have bought is not gold, but a frog, nourished in the breast of my pleasure. Then separate the body from the soul, and you will see that it will immediately fly to my breast of delight, where it was nourished.'

9- To whom I answer: 'Because the frog is horrible to look at, has a horrible voice, and is poisonous to the touch, and does not bring me anything good or pleasure, but to you, in whose breast it was nursed, let it be your own, because it is yours by right. Therefore, when the door is open, that is, when the soul is separated from the body, it will immediately fly to you, remaining with you without end.'

10- For such is the soul of him of whom I am speaking to you. For she is like the most wretched frog, full of all filthiness and pleasure, nourished in the breast of the devil. To whose coffin, that is to say, his body, now approaching by the approach of death, which hangs on the four hinges of the fall, because his body subsists on four, namely, strength, beauty, wisdom, and sight, all of which are now beginning to fail him.

11- And when her soul is separated from her body, she will immediately fly to the devil, on whose milk she was nourished, because she forgot my love, by which I took her punishment, which she deserved, on her behalf. For he does not repay me my love for my love, but moreover takes away from me my justice, because he ought to serve me, who redeemed her, rather than another. But she delights more in the devil.

12- The voice of his prayer is to me like the voice of a frog, the sight of him is abominable in my sight, his hearing will never hear my joy nor his touch poisoned my deity. However, because I am merciful, and his soul, even though it is impure, if someone would still repent and consider it, if there was any contrition in it and a good will, and if he would thrust into his mind the sharpest and fiercest lance, that is, the fear of my district judgment, he would still find my grace. if he wanted to agree.

13- If there was no contrition or charity in him, if someone nevertheless pricked him with biting rebuke and harsh criticism, there would still be hope in him, because as long as the soul lived with the body, my mercy was open to all. Behold, therefore, because I died for charity, and no one repays me charity, but takes away my justice, because it would be just, that men should live better the more labor they were redeemed.

14- But now they want to live the worse, the more bitterly I will redeem them, the more trustingly they want to sin, the more I show them the abominable sin. Therefore, see and consider, that I am not angry without cause, because they turn my grace into wrath for themselves. For I have redeemed them from sin, and they are now more involved in sin.

15- You, then, my bride, return to me that which you hold, that is, save your soul clean for me, because I died for her for this reason, so that you could save her clean for me."

Chapter 22

The most sweet question of the Mother to the bride and the humble answer of the bridegroom to the Mother, and the useful replication of the Mother to the bride and the departure of the good among the bad.

1- The mother spoke to her son's bride, saying: "You are my son's bride. Tell me what you have in mind and what you want!" To which the bride answered: "You know well, lady, because you know everything." And then the blessed Virgin said: "Even if I know everything, I will know you by speaking to those who hear and stand by."

2- And the bride said: "Two things," she said, "I am afraid, madam. First, for the sins that I do not weep for or redeem, as I would. Secondly, I am saddened by the fact that the enemies of your children are many." Then the virgin Mary answered: "On the contrary, first I give you three remedies. First, consider that all that have a spirit, such as the frog and other animals, sometimes have inconveniences, and yet their spirit does not live forever, but dies with the body. But your soul and all man lived forever.

3- Secondly, think of the mercy of God, because no man is so sinful, if he has asked with a purpose of amendment and contrition, that his sin may not be forgiven. Thirdly, think how great is the glory of the soul that has lived with God and in God without end.

4- Against the second, namely that the enemies of God are many, I will give you three remedies. First, consider that your God and your Creator and theirs is the judge over them, and they will never again judge him, although he patiently endures their malice for a time. Secondly, that they are the children of damnation, and how great and intolerable it will be for them to burn forever.

5- They are the worst heirs, who will lose their inheritance, but their children will receive their inheritance. But perhaps you will say: 'So it is not necessary to preach to them?' Of course! Consider that there are often good among the bad. And adopted children sometimes turn away from good, like that prodigal son who went to another distant country and lived badly.

6- But they themselves sometimes turn back to their father in remorse through preaching and will be more accepting than before they were sinners. That is why it is necessary to preach to them more, because although the preacher sees almost everyone as bad, he still considers with himself: 'Perhaps some of them are the future children of my Lord. I will therefore preach to them.' This preacher will have the best reward.

7- Thirdly, consider that the wicked are allowed to live as a trial of the good, so that those who are exasperated by their behavior may be rewarded with patience and fruit, as you will be able to understand by the example. For the rose smells sweetly, is beautiful to the sight, soft to the touch, and yet grows only among thorns, which are rough to the touch, ugly to the sight, and smelling nothing good.

8- Even so, good and just men, although they are gentle in patience, beautiful in character, gentle in their good example, yet they cannot make progress or be tested except among the wicked. And sometimes even the thorn protects the rose, lest it be plucked before it is ripe. Thus the evil is an occasion for the good, that they may not exceed in sins, when they are restrained by their malice, that they may not be dissolved by immoderate lechery or other sin.

9- Even so, wine is never served well in its goodness unless it is in the field, nor can the good and the just stand and prosper in virtue unless they are tried by tribulations and persecutions of the wicked. Therefore, bear with pleasure the enemies of my son, and think that he himself is their judge, and that if justice were such that they should all be destroyed, he could well destroy them in a moment. Therefore, bear with them as long as he bears with them!"

Chapter 23

Christ's words to the bride about the false man, who is called the enemy of God, and as much as possible about the hypocrite, and his full description of his properties.

1- He appears to men as a man well-dressed, strong and handsome, and active in the battle of his master, but when the helmet is removed from his head, he is loathsome to look at and useless for work. For his brain appears to be bare. He has ears in his forehead, eyes in the back of his head. His nose was cut off. His whole body contracted like that of a dead man. His jaw on the right side, together with the jaw and half of the lip, had all fallen off, so that nothing remained of the right side but only the throat, which appeared naked.

2- His chest is full of worms, and his arms are like two serpents. His heart is filled with the worst scorpion, his back is like burnt coal. His bowels are fetid and rotten, like flesh abounding in health, his feet dead and useless for walking. But what do these things mean, I will tell you.

3- He appears to men to be such, outwardly adorned with good manners and wisdom, and active in my honor, but it is by no means so. For if the helmet were removed from his head, that is to say, if he were to be shown to men as he is, he would be the most despicable of all. Indeed, his brain is naked, because the stupidity and levity of his behavior show by quite obvious signs that he is unworthy of such an honor among good men. For if he had understood my wisdom, he would have understood that he ought to be clothed with so much more austere conversation before others, with which he exalts himself with greater honor before others.

4- He has ears on his forehead, because instead of the humility which he ought to have in dignity and to shine in the rest, he does not want anything but to hear his own praise and honor, and for this he takes upon himself pride, whence he wants to be called great and good by all.

5- He has eyes in the back of his head, because his thinking is all about the present and not about the eternal, all about how it pleases men and what the usefulness of the flesh requires and not how it pleases me and benefits souls.

6- His nose was cut off, because discretion was taken away from him, by which he distinguishes between sin and virtue, between temporal and eternal honor, between eternal and eternal pleasures, between these modest and eternal pleasures.

7- His genes are contracted, that is to say, all the shame that he ought to have towards me, and the beauty of the virtues with which he pleased me, is completely as if dead to me. Because it is shame for men to sin, but nothing for me.

8- The other part of the jaw and lip had fallen, so that nothing remained but the throat, because the imitation of my works and the preaching of my words with fervent prayer had already fallen into him, so that nothing remained in him but the throat of his throat. But the imitation of good men, and the repetition of secular business, seem to them to be entirely healthy and beautiful.

9- His chest is full of worms, because in his chest, where there ought to be the memory of my passion and the memory of my works and those of my teachers, there are temporal cares and the greed of the world, which bite his consciousness like worms, so that he does not think of spiritual things.

10- In his heart, where I would like to dwell and where my charity should sit, sits the worst scorpion, who stings his tail and flatters his face, because from his mouth comes speech that is quite flattering and reasonable, but his heart is full of injustice and deceit, because he did not care, that the Church, to whom it presides, would be destroyed, if he could accomplish his will.

11- His arms are like serpents, because by his malice he extends himself to the simple, calling them to him with simplicity, but miserably supplanting them when he receives the opportunity. Then, like a snake, he twists himself in a circle, because he hides his malice and iniquity, so that hardly any people can detect his cunning.

12- This one is like the vilest snake in my sight, because just as a snake is more hateful than all animals, so this one is uglier than all of me, because he destroys my justice and considers me like a man who does not want to take revenge.

13- His back is like coal, but it ought to be like ivory, because his works ought to be stronger than others and cleaner, that he may bear the weak by patience and by his life a good example.

14- But now he is like coal, because he is too weak to negotiate a single word for my honor except for the sake of utility properly. However, he seems to be strong for the world. Therefore, when he thinks he is standing, he will fall, because he is so ugly and dead in the sight of me and of my saints as coal.

15- His insides are a stench, because his thoughts and affections stink in my sight like dead flesh, the stench of which no one can bear. Thus, none of the saints can bear him, but all turn their faces away from him and seek judgment upon him.

16- His feet are dead. For his two affections towards me have two feet, namely, the will to make amends and the will to do good. But these feet are completely dead in him, because all the marrow of charity is consumed in him, and nothing remains but the bones of induration. And so he stands before me. But as long as the soul is with the body, it can find my mercy."

17- Saint Laurence appeared, saying: "When I was in the world, I had three things: self-control, mercy to my neighbor, and love to God. Therefore, I fervently preached the word of God, wisely distributed goods to the Church, and joyfully endured beatings, fire and death."

18- But this bishop tolerates and conceals the intemperance of the clergy, he spends generously on the goods of the Church for many years, he has charity for himself and his people. Therefore I make it known to him that the lightest cloud had already ascended into the sky, which the torches obscured, so that it might not be seen by many.

19- Indeed, this cloud is the prayer of the mother of God for the Church, which the torches of covetousness and indolence and lack of justice overshadow in such a way that the gentleness of the mercy of the mother of God is not able to enter the hearts of the wretched.

20- For this reason, let the cicius bishop turn himself to divine charity, correcting himself and his subjects by admonishing them by example and words, and exhorting them to better things. Otherwise, he will cut off the hand of the judge and his church will be purified by fire and sword and will be afflicted with robbery and tribulation to such an extent that for a long time there will be no one to comfort it.

Chapter 24

The words of God the Father before the host of heaven and the response of the Son and Mother to the Father to obtain grace for the daughter.

1- The father spoke, in the hearing of the whole army of heaven, saying: "I complain to you that I gave my daughter over to a man who afflicts her excessively and binds her feet with a wooden club so that all the marrow comes out of her feet." To which the son answered: "She is she, father, whom I redeemed with my blood and betrothed to me, but now she has been violently kidnapped."

2- Then the mother spoke, saying: "You are my God and my Lord, and the members of your son were blessed in my body, who is your true son and my true son. For I denied you nothing on earth. Have mercy on your daughter because of my prayers!"

3- After this the angels spoke, saying: "You are our Lord and in you we have every good thing and we do not need anyone but you. When your bride came from you, we all congratulated ourselves. But now we could be rightfully saddened, because she was delivered into the hands of the worst, who took her He confounds with all meanness and reproach. Therefore, pity him because of your great mercy, because his misery is too great, and there is no one who can console and deliver it but you, Lord God Almighty."

4- Then the father answered his son, saying: "Son, your complaint is my complaint, your word is my word, your works are my works, you in me and I in you inseparably. Let your will be done!"

5- Then he said to the mother of the son: "Because you denied me nothing on earth, therefore I will deny you nothing in heaven. Your will will be done."

6- And he said to the angels: "You are my friends and the flame of your charity burns in my heart. I will show mercy to my daughter because of your prayers."

Chapter 25

The words of the creator to the bride, how his justice supports the evil three times and his mercy spares the evil three times.

1- I am the creator of heaven and earth. You would wonder, my bride, why I am so patient with evil. This is because I am compassionate. For my justice suffers them threefold and my mercy spares them threefold.

2- First, my justice suffers them, so that their time may be fully completed. For just as a just king, having some prisoners in prison, if he complains to him why they are not put to death, answers, 'because the general convention has not yet come, where they can be heard for greater caution' their malice.

3- Did I not long ago foretell the rejection of Saul, before he became known to men? I endured him for a long time, so that his malice might be shown to others. Secondly, because the wicked have done some good works, for which they must be rewarded to the last point, so that there is not some little good that they have done for me, for which they are not repaid, so that they may receive their reward here.

4- Thirdly, that the honor of God and his patience might be manifested, therefore I endured Pilate, Herod, and Judas, when they were nevertheless condemned. Therefore, if anyone complains about why I support him and him, let him consider Judas and Pilate.

5- My mercy also spares evil men threefold. First, because of excessive charity. For the eternal punishment is long. Therefore, for the sake of the greatest charity, I support them to the last point, so that the punishment from the long prolongation of time may begin more slowly for them.

6- Secondly, that their nature may be consumed in vices. For by sin the nature is consumed, lest they should feel that temporal death would be more bitter if their nature were fresher. For recent nature makes death more protracted and bitter.

7- Thirdly, to the advancement of good things and the conversion of some evil ones. For when good men and the righteous are afflicted by the wicked, either it is profitable for the good and the righteous themselves to make reference to sin, or to acquire greater merit.

8- In the same way, evil sometimes lives for the sake of good. For the wicked, when they consider the fall and iniquity of some wicked men, think to themselves, saying: 'What profit is there for us to follow them?' and 'When the Lord is so patient, it is better to be converted.'

9- And so sometimes they turn away from me, because they are averse to doing such things, as those evil people do, their conscience telling them not to do such things. Hence it is said that a person stung by a scorpion, if he is stung with oil in which another snake has died, is healed.

10- Thus, sometimes the wicked, seeing the fall of another, is rebuked, and, considering the other's iniquity and vanity, is healed.

Chapter 26

The words of praise of the angelic host to God and of the generation of children, if the first parents had not sinned, and how God showed miracles through Moses to the people and later himself to us in his coming, etc., and about the corruption of this time of physical marriage and about the conditions of spiritual marriage.

1- The angelic army was seen standing before God and the whole army said: "Praise be to you, Lord God, and honor, who are and who were without end! We are your servants and for a threefold reason we praise and honor you. First, because you created us, we would rejoice with you, and you gave us an indescribable light, with which we would rejoice forever.

2- Secondly, because in thy goodness and in thy stability all things were created and persist, and all things stand at thy will and abide in thy word. Thirdly, because you created man, for whom you took humanity. From which is our greatest joy and the most chaste of your mother, who deserved to bear you, whom the heavens could not contain and contain.

3- Therefore, be your glory and blessing above all for the angelic dignity with which you have exalted yourself with so much honor! May your perpetual eternity and stability be above all that is stable and can be! May your love be upon the man whom you have created!

4- You, Lord, alone are to be feared for your great power, you alone are to be desired for all your love, you alone are to be loved for your steadfastness. Therefore, praise be to you without end and without ceasing for ever and ever, amen!"

5- Then the Lord answered: "You honor me worthily for all creatures. But say, why do you praise me for a man, when he himself provoked me to anger more than all creatures! For I created him more excellent than all the creatures of the underworld and I suffered for no one so unworthily and no I was so carelessly redeemed as a man.

6- Or what creature does not keep its order except man? But he is more troublesome to me than the rest of the creatures. For as I created you for my praise and glory, so I made man for my honor. For I gave him a body like a spiritual temple, in which I placed a soul like a beautiful angel, because the soul of man is like an angel of virtue and strength.

7- In which temple I, his God and creator, was a third party, in which he was delighted and enjoyed. Then I made for him another temple of his own rib, similar to this one.

8- But now, O my bride, because of whom these things are happening, you can complain: 'How could children be born from them if they had not sinned?' I answer you: Certainly, from divine love and mutual love and intermingling of the sexes, by which both were in turn ignited, the blood of charity would fecundate in the woman's body without any foul pleasure, and thus the woman would become fruitful.

9- Then, having conceived a child without sin and voluptuous delight, I would send forth the soul from my divinity, and thus without pain she would bear the child and give birth. The child who was born would immediately be perfect like Adam. Man despised this honor when he agreed with the devil and desired a greater honor than I had given him.

10- And when the disobedience was done, my angel came upon them, and they were ashamed of their nakedness, and immediately they felt the lust of the flesh, and suffered hunger and thirst. Then they also missed me, whom, when they had them, did not feel hunger or any pleasure of the flesh or blushing, but I alone was to them all good and all sweetness and perfect delight.

11- And when the devil was rejoicing at their destruction and fall, I, moved with pity over them, did not leave them, but showed them threefold mercy. For I clothed them naked and gave them bread from the ground. For the lust, which the devil raised in them by their increased disobedience, I gave their souls in their seed through my deity. And whatever the devil suggested to them for evil, I turned all this to their good.

12- Then I showed them the way of living and worshiping me and allowed them to mix lawfully, although before my permission and instruction they were afraid to join. Similarly, when Abel was killed, when they mourned and abstained for a long time, I, moved with compassion, comforted them. And then they, knowing my will, began again to be united and to beget children. From whose descendants I myself, their creator, promised that I would be born.

13- And when the malice of the children of Adam increased, I then showed my justice to sinners but mercy to my elect, whom I appeased and saved them from perdition and exalted them, because they kept my precepts and believed my promises.

14- And when the time of mercy came, I showed my wonders through Moses. For I saved my people according to my promise. I gave them manna and I prayed for them in a pillar of cloud and fire, I gave them my law and showed them my secrets and the future through my prophets.

15- And after this I, who created all things, chose for myself a virgin, born of father and mother, from whom I assumed human flesh, and from her I was designed to be born without intercourse and sin, so that, just as those first children in paradise should have been born in the mystery of divine charity and out of mutual love and love of procreation, without any foul pleasure, so my deity received humanity from a virgin woman without intercourse and injury to her virginity.

16- When then the true God and man came in the flesh, I fulfilled the law and all the scriptures, as it had previously been prophesied about me, and I began a new law, because the old one was strict and hard to bear and was nothing but a figure of things to come. For in that ancient law it was lawful for one to have several wives, lest the posterity should pass without children, or that they should not mingle with the nations.

17- But in my new law it is prescribed for one husband to have only one wife, and it is forbidden for her to have more than one wife while she is alive. Whoever, therefore, is united by divine love and divine fear for the sake of the child to be received, these are the spiritual temples in which I desire to dwell thirdly.

18- But the people of this time are united by the reason of the seven. First, because of the beauty of the face; , for the sixth reason of raising children, not to be nourished by God or in good works, but for distinctions and honors; seventhly, they meet for the sake of lust, and in the desire of lust, like cattle.

19- These come with one agreement and concord before the doors of my church, whose affections and inner thoughts are entirely contrary to mine, and they prefer their will, which is to please the world, to my will. For if all their thoughts were towards me, and they committed their will into my hands, and accepted the marriage with my fear, then I would consent to them, and would be third with them.

20- But now my consent, which I ought to be their head, is absent, because lust is in their heart and not my love. Then they proceed to my altar, where they hear that they must be one heart and one soul, but then my heart flees from them, because they have no warmth from my heart and no taste of my flesh.

21- For they complained of the heat, which would quickly perish, and they complained of the flesh, which the worms were about to eat. Therefore, such are united without the bond of God the Father and his union and without the love of the Son and without the consolation of the Holy Spirit.

22- But when the spouses come to bed, then my spirit immediately departs from them and an unclean spirit approaches, because they do not meet except for the sake of lust, and nothing else is discussed or thought about between them. Nevertheless, my mercy is still with them, if they are converted. For out of much charity I send into their seed a living soul, created by my power, and sometimes I grant that good children may sometimes be born of bad parents. More often, however, bad children are born of bad parents, because such children imitate the iniquity of their parents as far as they can and would imitate more if they were permitted by my patience.

23- For such a couple will never see my face unless they repent. For no sin is so great that penance is not diluted. Therefore I turned to a spiritual marriage, such as God should have with a chaste body and a chaste soul. For there are found seven other good things, contrary to the previously mentioned evils.

24- For there it is not desired any form or beauty of the body, nor the sight of pleasant things, but only the sight and love of God; secondly, to possess nothing except where they live, only for necessity, nothing for superfluity; thirdly, they avoid idle and scurrilous words; fourthly, they do not care to see their friends or parents, but I am their love and desire.

25- Fifthly, they desire to maintain humility inwardly in conscience and outwardly in habit. Sixthly, they have the will to never want to be luxurious. Seventhly, they beget sons and daughters to their God through good conversation and a good example and through the preaching of spiritual words.

26- These then stand at the doors of my Church, when they observe the inviolable faith, where they assent to me and I to them. Indeed, they proceed to my altar and are spiritually delighted with my body and blood. In whose pleasure they desire to be one heart and one flesh and of one will, and I, true God and man, mighty in heaven and on earth, will be a third party with them, who will fill their hearts.

27- Those temporary spouses begin to lust after their spouses in lust like cattle, and worse than cattle. But these spiritual spouses begin in divine love and divine fear, caring to please no one but me. The evil spirit fills and excites them to the pleasure of the flesh, in which there is nothing but stench, but these are filled with my spirit and kindled by the fire of my charity, which will never fail them.

28- I am one God, triune in persons, one in substance with the Father and the Holy Spirit. For just as it is impossible to separate the Father from the Son and the Spirit from both, and just as it is impossible to separate heat from fire, so it is impossible to separate such spiritual spouses from me without being a third party with them. For my body was once wounded in passion and died, but it will never again be wounded or die.

29- Thus, they will never die from me, who are incorporated in me with right faith and perfect will. For wherever they stand, sit, or walk, I am always third with them."

Chapter 27

The Mother's words to the bride, how the three are in the dance and how this world is signified by the dance, and about the Mother's tribulation in Christ's death.

1- The Mother of God spoke to the bride, saying: "My daughter, I want you to know that, where there is a dance, there are three things, namely, empty flattery, an overflowing voice, and superfluous labor. But when someone sorrowful or sad enters the house of the choir, then his friend, Leticia, being in that dance, seeing her friend coming sad and distraught, let Leticia at once separate herself from the dance, and condole with her friend in sorrow.

2- This dance is this world, which is always desired by concern, which to foolish men seems to be a lethargy. In which world there are three things: vain flattery, scurrilous words, useless labor, because everything by which a man labors he leaves behind him. But he who is in the dance of this world, let him consider my labor and pain, and sympathize with me, that I was isolated from all the pleasures of the world, and separate himself from the world. For in the death of my son I was like a woman, having her heart fastened with five spears.

3- For the first lance was shameful and shameful nakedness, because I saw my chaste and most powerful son standing naked at the pillar and having no covering. The second was his accusation. For they accused him, saying that he was a traitor and a liar and even a plotter, whom I knew to be just and truthful and who had offended no one or wanted to offend.

4- My third lance was his crown of thorns, which so savagely pierced his most holy head, that blood flowed into his mouth and into his beard and into his ears. The fourth lance was the plaintive voice on the cross, with which he cried out to the Father, saying: 'O Father, why have you forsaken me?' As if he wanted to say: 'Father, there is no one to have mercy on me but you.' The fifth lance that pierced my heart was his most bitter death.

5- For from how many veins his precious blood came forth, as if my heart had been pierced with so many spears. The veins of his hands and feet were pierced, and the pain of the pierced sinews came inconsolably to his heart, and from his heart again to the sinews; life was prolonged among pains.

6- And when death was approaching, his heart would break with an intolerable pain, then immediately all his limbs trembled, and his head, which was leaning against his back, lifted itself a little.

7- The closed eyes were half-opened, as if half-opened. His mouth was likewise opened, and his tongue was seen to be bloody. The fingers and arms, which were somehow contracted, were stretched out. And with a spirit of surrender he bowed his head to his breast. The hands submitted to the place of the wounds a little. The feet supported the greater weight.

8- Then my hands were dry. The eyes were darkened and the face pale as if dead. The ears heard nothing. My mouth could not speak. My feet also swayed, and then my body fell to the ground. And when I rose from the earth, when I saw my son despised by the leper, I put all my will to him, knowing that everything had been done according to his will and could not have been done except by his permission, and I thanked him for everything.

9- And Leticia was mixed with a certain miscegenation, because I saw that he who had never sinned out of such charity was willing to suffer such things for sinners. Therefore, whoever is in the world, let him consider what I was like at the death of my son, and always keep it in mind!"

Chapter 28

The words of the Lord to the bride, an indication of how someone had come before his tribunal to be judged, and of the terrible and horrible sentence brought against him by God and by all the saints.

1- The bride saw God as if he were angry, who said: "I am without beginning and without end. There is no change with me, neither years nor days. But all the time of this world is with me, as if it were one hour or a moment.

2- Everyone who sees me sees and understands everything that is in me. But since you, my bride, are corporeal, therefore you cannot perceive and know like a spirit. Therefore, for your sake, I will tell you what has been done.

3- I sat as if in judgment, because all judgment was given to me, and someone came to be judged before the tribunal. To him the voice of the Father rang out, saying to him: 'Woe to you, because you were ever born', not because he repented that God had made him, but as one is wont to grieve for another by pitying him.

4- Then the voice of the Son answered: 'I shed my blood for you and accepted the most bitter penalty for you; for you are completely alienated from this, and it has nothing to do with you.' The voice of the Spirit says:

5- I inquired into all the corners of his heart, if by any chance I might find some softness in his heart and charity, but the coldest is like frost, the hardest like stone; there is nothing for me to do with him.'

6- Hey, the three voices were not heard because they were three gods, but because of you, my bride, they were made, because you could not understand this mystery otherwise. Then these three voices of the aforesaid, that is to say, of the Father and of the Son and of the Holy Spirit, were united at once into one voice only. That voice thundered thus, saying: 'The kingdom of heaven is not due to you at all.'

7- The mother was silent in mercy and did not open her mercy, because he was unworthy to be judged by her. And all the saints cried out with one voice, saying: 'This is divine justice, that he should be a perpetual exile from your kingdom and joy.'

8- And then all those who were in purgatory said: 'There is no punishment so bitter with us that it is sufficient to punish your sins. For you are required to carry larger guns; therefore, you will be kidnapped by us.' And then he himself, who was to be judged, cried out with a terrible voice, saying: 'Woe, woe to the seeds that came together in my mother's womb, from whom I was formed.'

9- Secondly, he also cried out: 'Cursed', he said, 'be the hour in which my soul was united with the body, and cursed be he who gave body and soul!' A third cried out: 'Cursed be that hour in which the living came forth from the mother's womb!'

10- Then there came against him three horrible voices from hell, saying: 'Come to us, cursed soul, as if you were flowing to perpetual death and endless life!' Secondly, they cried: 'I have come, cursed soul, empty to our malice! For there will be none of us who will not fill you with his malice and punishment.'

11- Thirdly, they cried: 'Come, cursed soul, heavy as a stone, which always sinks and never reaches the bottom where it rests! Thus, you will descend deeper than us into the depths, so that you will not be able to stand before you come into this abyss.'

12- And then the Lord said: 'Therefore as a man, having several wives and seeing the fall of one, turns himself away from her and turns himself to others who stand and congratulates himself with them, so I turn my face away from him and mercy, and turn myself to my servants and servants, and rejoice with them.

13- Therefore, when you heard of his fall and misery, I therefore became more sincere to myself, as I showed greater mercy to you! Flee the world and its lust! Did I suffer so bitterly for the sake of the glory of the world, or because I could not finish it more quickly and easily? Of course I could.

14- But justice demanded so that, as a man had sinned in all his members, so he had to be satisfied in all. Because of this, the deity, being compassionate to man, was kindled with such love for one virgin, that he assumed humanity from her, in which humanity God would endure all the punishment that man was held to have.

15- Therefore, if out of charity I have accepted your punishment upon me, stand, as my servants stand, in true humility, so that you may be ashamed of nothing, fear nothing but me! I guarded your mouth, so that, if it were my will, you would never want to speak. Do not grieve over temporal things, because they are transitory, and I can enrich whom I will and impoverish. Therefore, my bride, put your trust entirely in me!"

16- This man was a noble, a canon, and a subdeacon, who, having obtained a false dispensation, betrothed a virgin for a long time. But being prevented by a sudden death, he did not obtain what he desired.

Chapter 29

The Virgin's words to her daughter about two ladies, one of whom was named Pride and the other Humility, by which the sweetest Virgin is designated, and about the meeting of the Virgin with her loved ones at the time of her death.

1- The Mother of God speaks to the son's bride, saying: "There are two, sir. One is that which has no special name, because it is unworthy of a name; the other is Humility, which is called Mary. Over the first, the devil himself is the master, because he dominates himself.

2- His soldier said to this lady: 'O lady, I am ready to do whatever I can for you, so long as I enjoy your intercourse once. For I am strong in strength, great in heart, I fear nothing, and I am ready to go to death for you.' To whom she answered: 'My lord, your charity is great. But I sit in a lofty seat, and I have but one seat, and between us there are three porters.

3- The first gate is so narrow that, whatever a man has in his body, if he enters through it, everything is broken and taken away. The second is so sharp that it stings even to the nerves. The third gate is so burning that there is no respite from the ardor, but whoever enters through it will immediately melt as you are.

4- But I sit sublimely, and whoever wants to sit with me, since I have only one seat, will fall to the greatest chaos under me.' To whom the devil answered: 'I will give my life for you, because it is the least chance for me.'

5- This lady is Pride, to whom he who wishes to reach must enter as if through three gates. He enters the first gate, who gives all for the praise of men and for pride. And if he has nothing, he uses all his will, how he can be proud and praised. The second gate is entered by him who, whatever he labors and whatever he does, gives all his time and thoughts and all his strength to this, in order to perfect his pride.

6- And even if he could hand over his flesh to be torn for the sake of honor and division, he would gladly do it. He enters the third gate, who never rests and is never silent, and who burns like a fire, how can he attain any honor or pride of the world. But when he has obtained what he desires, he cannot long remain in the same state, but falls miserably. Nevertheless, pride remains in the world.

7- "But I," said Mary, "and I am most humble, I sit in a spacious seat and above me there is no sun, nor moon, nor stars, nor even clouds, but a wonderful and inestimable serenity of brightness, proceeding from the beauty of the glorious divine majesty. Below me there is not even earth or stones, but incomparable rest in the power of God. There is no wall or walls beside me, but a glorious army of angels and holy souls.

8- And although I sit thus sublimely, yet I hear my friends, who are on earth, pouring out groans and tears to me every day. I see their labors and their efficiency greater than those who fight for their lady pride. Therefore, I will visit them and place them with me in my seat, because it is spacious and can accommodate them all well. But they could not yet come to me nor sit with me, because there are still two walls between us, through which I will confidently lead them to come to my seat.

9- The first wall is the world, which is the frame. Therefore, my servants in the world will be comforted through me. The second wall is death. Therefore, I, their dearest lady and mother, will bow down to them and meet them in death, so that even in death itself they may have consolation and refreshment, and I will place them with me in the seat of heavenly joy, so that they may eternally rest in the arms of love with everlasting and eternal glory with immense exultation."

Chapter 30

The Lord's words of great charity to the bride about the multiplication of false Christians to Christ's crucifixion and how, if it were possible, he is still ready to accept death again for sinners.

1- I am God, who created all things for the benefit of man, that they might serve man and build him up. But man uses all that I have created for his benefit to his own detriment. Moreover, he cares less about God and loves him less than the creature.

2- The Jews inflicted on me three kinds of punishments in my Passion: first, the tree, to which I was fastened and scourged and crowned; secondly, the iron with which they fastened my hands and feet; a third drink, with which they made me drink. Then they blasphemed that I was a fool because of death, which I willingly endured, and called me a liar because of my teaching.

3- Such are now multiplied in the world, and few give me comfort. For they impale me on a tree through the will to sin, they scourge me through impatience, because no one can bear one word for me. And they crown me with the thorn of their pride, with which they want to be more proud of me. They pierce my hands and feet with the iron of hardness, because they boast of sin and harden themselves, so that they do not fear me.

4- They offer me tribulation because of my anger, and because of the suffering I suffered, they call me a liar and a fool. For I am able to drown them and the whole world for their sins, if I would. And then, if I drowned them, those who remained would serve me out of fear, but this would not be justice, because a man ought to serve me out of charity.

5- But if I should personally come among them, visible, their eyes would not bear to see me, nor their ears to hear me. For how could a mortal man see an immortal? Indeed, out of charity I would gladly die again for a man, if it were possible."

6- Then appeared the blessed virgin Mary, to whom the son said: "What do you want, my mother, my chosen one?" And she said: "Have mercy on your creatures, my son, because of your love!" And he answered: "I will show mercy once more for your sake."

7- Then the Lord spoke to his bride, saying: "I am your God and the Lord of the angels. I am the Lord over death and life. I also want to dwell in your heart. See, how much love I have for you!"

8- The heavens and the earth and all that is in them cannot contain me, and yet I want to dwell in your heart, which is only a small piece of flesh. Who then will you be able to fear and need, when you have within you the most powerful God, in whom is all good?

9- Therefore, in the heart, which is my habitation, there must be three things: a bed in which we rest, a seat in which we sit, a light by which we are enlightened. Therefore, let there be a bed of rest or tranquility in your heart, so that you may rest from the evil thoughts and desires of the world. And always consider eternal joy!

10- The seat must be the will to stay with me, even if it happens that I leave. For it is contrary to nature to always stand. For he always stands, who always has the will to be with the world and never to sit with me. Light, or light, must be the faith by which you believe that I can do all things and that I am omnipotent overall.

Chapter 31

How the bride saw the most sweet virgin Mary decorated inestimably with a crown and other ornaments, and how the bridegroom, St. John the Baptist, declares what is signified by the crown, etc.

1- He saw the bride, the queen of heaven, the mother of God, having on her head an inestimable precious crown, and her hair spread over the shoulders of wonderful beauty, a golden robe shining with indescribable splendor, and a mantle of azure or the clearest color of the sky.

2- And when the bride was vehemently amazed at such a beautiful vision, and in such wonder she stood completely suspended in a sort of internal stupor, immediately appeared to her the blessed John the Baptist, who said to her:

3- "Listen carefully, what does this signify! The crown therefore signifies that she is queen and lady and the mother of the king of angels. Her long hair, that she is a most pure and immaculate virgin. She was burning and fervent with divine love both internally and externally.

4- And in his crown his son put seven lilies, and between these lilies he placed seven stones. Therefore, the first lily is his humility, the second fear, the third obedience, the fourth patience, the fifth stability, the sixth meekness, because he is gentle in giving to all who ask. The seventh is compassion in need. For in whatever need a man may be, if he calls upon her with all his heart, he will be saved.

5- Among these shining lilies his son placed seven precious stones. The first stone is singular virtue, because there is no virtue in any spirit or in any body which does not possess this same virtue more excellently.

6- The second stone is the most perfect purity, because that queen of heaven was so pure that not one spot of sin could ever be found in her from the beginning of her entry into the world until the last day of her death. Nor could all the devils find so much impurity in her that the point of a needle could be put into it. She was truly pure. For it was not fitting for a king to lie in glory except in a vessel most pure and clean and most chosen before all angels and men.

7- The third stone was her beauty, because God is continually praised by his saints for the beauty of the same mother, and the joy of the holy angels and all holy souls is filled by her beauty.

8- The fourth precious stone in the crown is the wisdom of the same virgin mother, because she is filled with all divine wisdom with God and from her all wisdom is filled and perfected.

9- The fifth stone is fortitude, because it is so strong with God that it can depress all things, whatever was created and made.

10- The sixth stone is also its brightness, which is so bright that the angels, who have eyes brighter than the light, are illuminated by it, and the demons do not dare to look into its brightness.

11- The seventh stone is the fullness of all delight, and also of spiritual sweetness, which is so full in it, that there is no joy that is not increased by it, no delight that is not made fuller and perfected by it and by its blessed vision, because it itself she was filled and filled with grace beyond all the saints. For she is the vessel of purity, in which lay the bread of the angels, and in which is all sweetness and beauty.

12- His son placed these seven stones among these seven lilies that were in his crown. Therefore, O bride of his son, honor and praise her with all your heart, because she is truly worthy of all praise and honor!"

Chapter 32

How the bride, forewarned by God's admonition, chose poverty for herself and refused divisions and carnality and from the truth revealed in her and from the notable tribes shown to her by Christ.

1- You must be like a man who leaves and like a man who gathers. For you must leave the divisions and gather the virtues, leave the accidents and gather the eternal, leave the visible and gather the invisible. For I will give you for the delight of the flesh the exaltation of the soul, for the joy of the world the joy of heaven, for the honor of the world the honor of the angels, for the vision of my parents the vision of God, for the possession of goods myself, the giver and creator of all things.

2- Tell me three things that I want from you! First, if you want to be rich at this age or poor." And she answered: "Lord, I would rather be poor, because the two do not do me any good except a certain concern and draw me back from your service."

3- "Tell me a second time, did you find in my words, which you heard from my mouth, anything reprehensible according to your heart or false?" And she: "Certainly not, because everything is according to reason."

4- "Thirdly, tell me whether you like the pleasure of the flesh that you had before, or the pleasure of the spirit that you have now!" And she answered: "I am ashamed in my heart to think of that former pleasure of the flesh, and it is now like poison to me, and more bitter now that I loved her more fervently than before. For I would rather die than ever return to her, and there is no comparison of that spiritual delight to her."

5- "Therefore," he said, "you prove in yourself that all that I have told you is true. Why then are you afraid or why are you worried, because I am prolonging the things that I told you to do? Consider the prophets, consider the apostles and the holy teachers! Have they found anything in me?" but the truth? Therefore, they cared not for the world nor for its concupiscence.

6- Or why did the prophets prophesy so far about the future, unless it was God's will that the words should first be known, and then the works should come, and that the unlearned should be taught to faith? Indeed, all the mysteries of my incarnation were previously known to the prophets, even the star that preceded the magicians, who, believing the words of the prophet, deserved to see what they believed, and having seen the star, they were immediately certified.

7- So now my words must first be announced and later, when the works come, they will be believed to be more evident.

8- I have shown you three. First, I proved the conscience of one, whose sin I had made manifest, by the most evident signs. But why? Could I not kill him personally? Or couldn't I drown him at a point if I wanted to? Of course I could.

9- But for the sake of the education of others and the plainness of my words, to show how just and patient I am, and how unhappy he is, who is dominated by the devil, therefore I still suffer him. For from the will which he has to be in sin, and from the delight in it, the power of the devil is so increased over him, that neither gentleness of words, nor austerity of threats, nor fear of hell can call him back.

10- And well worthily, because since he had always had the will to sin, even if he did not come forward to work, he would deservedly be delivered to the eternal devil. Because the smallest sin, whoever delights in it and does not correct it, is enough for him to perish.

REVELATIONS

11- I will show you two others. The devil tormented the body of another but was not in the soul; the other's conscience was overshadowed by his delusions, and yet it was not in his soul, nor had he power over it.

12- But perhaps you can complain: 'Aren't conscience and soul the same? Is it not then in the soul, when it is in consciousness?' No way. But just as the body has two eyes with which it sees, and though sight is taken away from them, the body can nevertheless be healthy by no means, so it is in the soul. For although the intellect and conscience are sometimes disturbed as to punishment, yet the soul is not always injured as to guilt. And therefore the devil prevailed in the consciousness of one, not in the soul.

13- I will show you a third, in whose soul and body the devil has complete dominion. Who, unless compelled by my power and special grace, will never be driven out of it nor come out of it. For from some men the devil comes out willingly and quickly, and from others only after being urged on and forced.

14- For the devil enters into some, either because of the fault of the parents, or because of some secret judgment of God, as if into children and the foolish; on some because of unbelief or some other sin. From these the demon willingly comes out, if it is cast out by those who know conspiracies or the art of casting out demons, if they themselves do such casting out for vainglory or for some temporal gain, because the devil has the power to enter into him who cast out, and into him again. from whom he was cast out, because there was no divine charity in any of them.

15- But from those whose soul and body he possesses completely, he never leaves except through my power. For just as vinegar, if mixed with the sweetest wine, infects the whole sweetness of the wine and is never separated from it, so also the devil does not come out of the soul of a man who possesses it, except by my power.

16- But what is this wine but the soul, which was sweetest to me above all creation, which was so dear to me, that I cut my sinews and caused my flesh to be torn to the ribs for it? And, before I lost her, I even received death for her.

17- This wine was stored in the waste, because I placed the soul itself in the body, in which it was kept as if in a closed vessel at my will. But mixed with this sweet wine is the worst vinegar, that is, the devil, whose malice is more acrid to me and more abominable than any vinegar.

18- This vinegar will be separated by my power from this man, whose name I tell you, so that in this I may show my mercy and wisdom, but in the former my judgment and justice."

19- The first was a nobleman and a proud singer, who, going to Jerusalem without permission from the pope, was seized by the devil. It is also said of this demoniac.

20- The second demoniac of the same chapter was a monk of the Cistercian order, whom the devil tormented so much that he could hardly be held by four. His tongue seemed to be drawn out like a cow, and the chains of his hands were invisibly broken. He was saved by Lady Bridget after a month and two days by the words of the Holy Spirit.

21- The third demoniac was the driver of Osgocia, who, when he was admonished to do penance, said to the admonisher: "Will the inhabitant of the house be able to sit where he pleases? The devil holds my heart and my tongue. How can I repent?" He who even cursed the saints of God died that very night without sacraments and confession.

Chapter 33

The words of the Lord's admonition to the bride about true and false wisdom and how good angels assist the good wise and the devil the evil wise.

1- Some of my friends are like my pupils, who have three things: firstly, an intelligent consciousness above the nature of the brain, secondly, wisdom without man, because I personally teach them within; thirdly, they are full of sweetness and divine love, with which they overcome the devil.

2- But on the contrary, men are now learning. First, they want to be knowledgeable for the sake of boasting, so that they may be called good clerics. Secondly, they want to be knowledgeable, so that they can have and wish to be divided. Thirdly, they want to be knowledgeable, so that they can obtain honors and dignities.

3- Therefore, when they go to their schools and enter, I leave them, because they themselves learn because of pride, and I taught them humility. They go in because of greed, and I had no place to lay my head. They enter in order to have dignities, insinuating that they are superior to others, and I was judged by Pilate and ridiculed by Herod.

4- Therefore, I will go away from them, because they do not learn my doctrine. But still, because I am gentle and good, I give to everyone what he asks. For he that asketh me bread, he shall have it. But to him shall be given straw.

5- But my friends themselves ask for bread, because they complain and learn divine wisdom, in which is my charity. But others ask for straw, that is, worldly wisdom. For as there is no use in straw, and the food of unreasonable animals, so in the wisdom of the world, which they complain of, there is no use, and no restoration to the soul except a small name and empty labor, because when a man dies, all his wisdom is annihilated and from by whom he was praised cannot be seen.

6- Wherefore I am like a great master, having many servants, who administer on the part of the master, which are necessary for all. Thus the angels of good and evil stand at my command.

7- But those who learn my wisdom, that is, to serve me, good angels administer to them, refreshing them with comfort and pleasant work. But the wise men of the world are assisted by evil angels, who inspire them with what they will, and shape them according to their will, and inspire thought with great effort.

8- However, if they looked at me, I would suffice to give them bread without toil and the world to satiety, of which they are never satisfied, because they turn sweet into bitter for themselves.

9- But you, my bride, must be like cheese, your body like a mold, in which the cheese will be formed until it has a moldy shape. Thus, your soul, which is as sweet and delicious to me as cheese, must be tested and purified for so long in the body, until body and soul are united in one and both hold one form of continence, so that the flesh obeys the spirit and the spirit governs the flesh to all power."

Chapter 34

Christ's teaching to the bride about the way of living and how the devil confesses to Christ that he loves the bride Christ himself above all things and about the question made by the devil to Christ, why he loved her so much, and about the love revealed by the devil that Christ has for the bride.

1- I am the creator of heaven and earth, who in the womb of a virgin was a true God and true man, who died and rose again and ascended into heaven.

2- You, my new bride, have come to an unknown place. It is therefore necessary for you to have four things: first, to know the language of the place, secondly, to have the proper clothes, thirdly, to know how to arrange the days and times according to the constitution of the place, and fourthly, to get used to new foods.

3- Thus you, since you have come from the instability of the world to stability, therefore you must also have a new speech, that is, abstinence from useless words and sometimes even from lawful ones because of the seriousness of silence and taciturnity.

4- Your clothes must be humble inwardly and outwardly, so that you neither exalt yourself as if you were sanctimonious to others inwardly, nor are you ashamed to show yourself humble outwardly before men.

5- The third regulation of your time is that, just as you had several times for the needs of the body, so now you have one time for the soul, so that you may never want to sin against me.

6- Fourthly, the new food is abstinence from gluttony and from dainties with all discretion, as nature can bear. For whatever is done with abstinence beyond the possibility of nature, I do not like it, because I require reasonable things and that pleasure should be tamed.

7- Then at the same moment the devil appeared. The Lord said to him: "You were created in me and you saw all justice in me. Answer me if this new bride is legitimately mine and with approved justice! Does he love something like me, or would he accept something in exchange for me?"

8- To whom the demon answered: "He loves nothing like you, and before he lost you, he would have endured all the punishment more if you had given him the strength to be patient."

9- I see, as it were, a burning bond descends from you into her, which so binds her heart that she thinks of or loves nothing else but you."

10- Then the Lord said to the devil: "Tell me, how does it sit in your heart, or how does it please you that I have so much love for her?"

11- And the devil said: "I," said he, "have two eyes, one corporeal, although I am not corporeal, with which I see temporal things so clearly, that nothing is so hidden, nothing so dark, that can hide itself from me."

12- The second eye is spiritual, with which there is no punishment so small that I do not see and understand, to which sin belongs.

13- And I do not see any sin so light and small, which has not been cleansed by penance. But although there are no members more susceptible to the eyes, yet I willingly suffered the two burning torches to penetrate my eyes without ceasing to this end, so that she could not see with her spiritual eyes.

14- I also have two ears, one bodily, with which no one speaks so secretly that I do not hear and know. The second is spiritual, by which no one thinks or feels about any sin so secretly that I will not hear of it unless it is removed by penance.

15- There is one punishment of hell, boiling as if it were a torrent, emanating with the most intense heat. I would willingly allow this to flow in and flow out without ceasing into my ears for this purpose, so that she could hear nothing with her spiritual ears.

16- I, too, have a spiritual heart, which I willingly suffered to be cut into pieces without ceasing and to be always renewed for execution for this purpose, so that its heart may grow cold in your love.

17- But now, since you are just, I ask you for one word, that you may answer me: Tell me, why do you love her so much, or why did you not choose for yourself someone more sanctified, more eloquent and more beautiful?"

18- To whom the Lord answered: "Because justice demanded so. Indeed, you were created in me and you saw all justice in me. Tell me, hearing this, what justice was, that you fell so badly, or what was your thinking then, when you fell!"

19- The devil answered: "I saw three things in you: I saw your glory and honor above all, and I thought of my glory. Therefore, being proud, I proposed not only to be equal to you, but to surpass you."

20- Secondly, I saw that you were stronger than all. That's why I wanted you to be stronger. Thirdly, I saw that they were to come, and since your glory and honor are without beginning and would be without end, I envied you and thought that I would gladly torture you with all the bitterest punishment for this, so that you might die. And I fell into such a thought. And therefore hell was made."

21- The Lord answered: "You asked me why I loved her so much. Certainly, because I change all your malice into good. For you, because you became proud and did not want me, your creator, to be equal, therefore I, humiliating myself in everything, gather sinners and I compare myself to them, giving them my glory.

22- Secondly, because you had such a weak desire that you wanted to be stronger than me, therefore I make sinners powerful over you and powerful with me.

23- Thirdly, because you envied me, I am so charitable that I would offer myself for all."

24- Then the Lord said: "Now, devil, your dark heart has been enlightened. Say, hearing this, what kind of love I have for her!" And the devil: "If it were possible," said he, "you would most willingly suffer one such punishment in each of your members in particular, such as you once suffered in all your members on the cross, before you lost them."

25- Then the Lord answered: "If, then, I am so merciful as to deny forgiveness to anyone who asks for it, humbly ask for mercy from me too, and I will give it to you."

26- To whom the devil answered: "I will do this by no means. For when I fell, for every sin, whether it was a useless thought or a word, a penalty was established, and each one of the spirits who fell will have his penalty.

27- Therefore, before I bend my knee before you, I would rather swallow all the punishments in me, as long as the mouth could be opened and closed for punishment, so that I would always be renewed for punishment."

28- Then the Lord said to his bride: "Look how hardened the ruler of the world is and how powerful against me because of my secret justice! Indeed, I could destroy him from my power in one point but I do him no greater injury than the good angel in heaven. But when his time has come, which is now drawing near, I will judge him with his followers.

29- Therefore, my bride, always proceed in good works! Love me with all your heart! Fear nothing but me! For I am lord over the devil and over all things, whatever they may be.

Chapter 35

The words of the Virgin to the bride, explaining her own pain in Christ's passion, and how the world was sold through Adam and Eve and redeemed through Christ and his virgin mother.

1- Mary spoke: "Consider, daughter, the suffering of my son! His members were to me as my members and as my heart. For he, as other children are wont to be in the womb of a mother, so was he in me. But he was conceived from the fervent love of divine love and others from the concupiscence of the flesh.

2- Whence well says John, his cousin brother: 'The word became flesh.' For by charity he himself came and was in me. But the word and charity did it for me. For he was to me as my own heart.

3- Therefore, when it was born from me, I felt that it was as if half my heart was born and went out of me. And when he himself suffered, I felt that my heart was at peace.

4- For as that which is half outside and half inside, and if that which is outside is pricked, the horse feels the pain which is inside, so I, when my son was scourged and pricked, as if my heart were scourged and pricked.

5- I was also closer to him in emotion and did not separate from him. I stood nearer to his cross, and as this stings more deeply, because it is nearer to the heart, so his pain was greater than the rest of me.

6- And when he looked at me from the cross and I at him, then tears flowed from my eyes as if from my veins. And when he himself saw me worn out with pain, he was so embittered by my pain, that all the pain of his wounds seemed to him to be asleep before my pain, which he saw in me.

7- Therefore I say boldly, because his pain was my pain, because his heart is my heart. For as Adam and Eve sold the world for one apple, so my son and I redeem the world as if with one heart. Therefore, my daughter, think what I was like at the death of my son, and it will not be too great for you to leave the world."

Chapter 36

The answer of the Lord to the angel, praying for the bride, that tribulation of body and soul be granted to the bridegroom, and that greater tribulations be given to those who are more perfect.

1- Angelo, praying for his Lord's bride, the Lord answered: "You are like a soldier of the Lord, who never put down his helmet because of weariness and who, because of fear, never took his eyes off the battlefield.

2- You are steady like a mountain, burning like a flame. You are so clean that there is no spot in you. You ask for mercy from my spouse. Although you know and see everything in me, yet, hearing this, tell me what kind of mercy you ask for him!

3- For mercy is threefold: one, by which the body is punished and the soul is spared, like my servant Job, whose flesh was given to all pains and his soul was spared; the second is mercy, by which body and soul are spared from punishment, like that king who was in all pleasures and had no pain either for body or soul while he lived in the world; The third is mercy, by which body and soul are punished, so that they may have tribulation in the flesh and pain in the heart, like Peter and Paul and other saints.

4- For there are three states of men in the world: one of those who fall into sins and rise again. I allow these sometimes to be tribulated to the body, so that they may be saved.

5- The second is of those who would gladly live eternally, so as to sin eternally, who have all their will towards the world, and if they sometimes do something for me, they do it with this intention, so that their temporal things may increase and prosper.

6- These are not given the punishment of the body nor the great pain of the heart, but they are released in their own power and of their own will, because for the smallest good that they have done for me, they will receive their reward here, to be crucified for eternity, because since the will is eternal to sin, the punishment it will be eternal to them.

7- The third state is those who are more afraid of sinning against me and offending my will than of any punishment. More and more they would be tormented for eternity by an intolerable punishment that they knowingly provoked me to anger.

8- To these is given tribulation of body and heart, like Peter and Paul and other saints, so that, whatever they have sinned in this world, they may make amends in the world, or they may be purified for a time for greater glory and as an example to others. I performed this threefold mercy in this kingdom with the three whose names are known to you.

9- Now, then, angel, my servant, what kind of mercy do you ask for my spouse?" And he said, "Soul," he said, "and of body, so that whatever he has sinned here, he may make amends in the world, and none of his sins may come to your judgment." The Lord answered: "Thy will be done!"

10- Then he spoke to the bride: "You are mine. Therefore, as I please, I will do with you. Love no one like me! Purify yourself constantly from sin every hour with the counsel of those to whom I have committed you! Conceal no sin! Let nothing go unchallenged! No sin, think lightly, no neglect!

11- For everything, whatever you neglect, I will bring to memory and judge. For no sin of yours will come into my judgment, because penance in your life will be punished. As for those for whom penance has not been done, they will either be purged in purgatory or by some other secret judgment of mine, unless they are redeemed here with satisfaction."

Chapter 37

The words of the mother to the bride, the presentation of the excellency of her son, and how Christ is now more severely crucified by the enemies, the bad Christians, than he was crucified by the Jews, and consequently, that such will be punished more severely and bitterly.

1- The mother said: "My son had three virtues. First, because no one had such a delicate body as he, because he was of the two best natures, namely, divinity and humanity, and so the world, which, just as in the clearest eye no spot is found, so neither some deformity could be found in his body.

2- The second good thing was that he never sinned. For other children sometimes bear the sins of their parents and their own; for he never sinned and yet bore the sins of all.

3- The third was that some die for the sake of God and a greater reward. But he was dying as much for his enemies as for me and his friends.

4- But when his enemies crucified him, they did four things to him: first, they crowned him with thorns, secondly, they pierced his hands and feet, thirdly, they threw him bile, fourthly, they pierced his side.

5- But now I complain that my son is crucified by his enemies, who are now in the world, more bitterly than the Jews crucified him then. For though you may say that he is impassive and cannot die, yet they crucify him with his own vices.

6- For just as a man insults and injures the image of an enemy of his, although he does not feel that the image has been inflicted, yet because of his evil will to injure the injurer is accused and judged for his work, so their vices, with which they spiritually crucify my son, are more abominable and graver to him than theirs , who crucified him in the body.

7- But perhaps you can complain: 'How did they crucify him?' Of course, first they put him on the cross which they had prepared for themselves, when they do not care about the commandments of their creator and Lord and dishonor him when he instructs them to serve him through his servants, and they themselves do this in contempt, as they please.

8- Then they crucify the right hand, when they hold justice for injustice, saying: 'Sin is not so grievous and hateful to God, as it is said, nor does God afflict anyone eternally but because of fear. For why should he redeem a man if he willed him to perish?

9- And because God forgives not the smallest sin unpunished, just as not the smallest good goes unrewarded, therefore their punishment will be eternal, because they have an eternal will to sin, which my son, who sees the heart, counts as a work. Because, as they have the will, so also, they would complete the work, if my son would allow it.

10- Then they crucify his left hand, when they turn virtue into vice, willing to sin until the end, saying: 'If we say at the end once, "Have mercy on me, God!", such is the mercy of God that we shall have forgiveness.'

11- This is not virtue, to wish to sin and not amend, to wish to have a premium without effort, unless there was a contrition in the heart, which he would willingly wish to amend, if he could before infirmity or some other hindrance.

12- Afterwards they crucify his feet, when they delight in committing sin, and not once do they think of the bitter punishment of my son, nor do they once thank him from the bottom of their hearts, saying: 'O how bitter was thy passion, O God! Praise be to thee for thy death!' This never comes out of their mouths.

13- Then they crown him with a crown of derision, when they mock his servants and consider it vanity to serve him. They give him gall to drink, when they rejoice and exult in sin. Not once did it enter their hearts, however great and how complex it was. They sting his side when they have the will to continue in sin.

14- I tell you the truth, and you will be able to say this to my friends, that they are such before my son, who judge him more unjustly, more unkind to his crucifixors, more impudent to his sellers, and a greater punishment is due to these than to them.

15- For Pilate knew well that my son had not sinned, nor was he worthy of any death. Nevertheless, because he feared the loss of temporal power and the sedition of the Jews, he judged as if he had sent my son to death.

16- But what would these people have to fear if they were to serve him? Or what would they lose of their honor and dignity if they honored him?

17- Therefore, these will be judged more seriously and are worse than Pilate in the sight of my son, because Pilate judged him because of the request and the will of others with some fear. But they judge him for their own advantage without fear, when they dishonor him for a sin from which, if they wished, they could abstain.

18- But they neither abstain from sin, nor are they ashamed of the sin they have committed, because they do not consider that they are unworthy of his benefits, to whom they do not serve.

19- Judas is worse, because Judas, having surrendered to the Lord, knew that God himself was good and that he had sinned grievously against him, but he despaired of himself and hastened his days to hell, believing himself to be living unworthy.

20- But they know well their sin, and yet they persist in it, having no remorse for it in their hearts, but they want to take the kingdom of heaven with a kind of violence and power, when they think that they have this not by works but by vain hope, which will be given to none but the laborer and the patient something for God

21- They are even worse than the crucified, because when they saw the good works of my son, namely that he raised the dead and cleansed the lepers, they thought to themselves:

22- Here he does unheard and unusual wonders, for he prostrates whom he wills with a single word, he knows our thoughts, he does whatever he wants. If he will have his process, we will all be subject to his power and will be his subjects.' Therefore, that they might not submit to him, they crucified him because of their enmity. For if they had known that he had been a king of glory, they would never have crucified him.

23- But they see his works every day and great wonders, they use his benefits and hear how they should serve him and come to him, but they think to themselves:

24- 'If all temporal things are to be abandoned, if his will and not ours is to be done, this is grave and intolerable.'

25- Therefore, despising his will, lest it should be above theirs, they crucify my son through indifference, adding sin upon sin against their conscience.

26- But these are worse than the crucifixion, because the Jews did it out of envy and because they did not know that he was God. But these know that he is God, and out of their own malice and presumption, for the sake of lust, they crucify him spiritually more bitterly than they carnally, because these were redeemed, they were not yet redeemed.

27- Therefore, bride, obey my son and fear him, because as he is merciful, so he is also just!

Chapter 38

The happy conversation between God the Father and the Son, and how the Father gave a new bride to the Son and the Son accepted her with gratitude, and how the bridegroom informs the bride about patience and simplicity by example.

1- The Father spoke to the Son: "I came with love to the virgin and took your true body from her. Therefore, you in me and I in you. As fire and heat are never separated, it will be impossible to separate deity from humanity."

2- The Son answered: "All glory and honor be to you, Father! Let your will be done in me and mine in you!"

3- The Father answered again: "Behold, my son, I assign this new bride to you as an egg to rule and nurture. Of which, as the possessor of the egg, you will have cheese to make and milk to drink and wool to clothe yourself with."

4- But you, bride, must obey him. For three things belong to you: you must be patient, obedient, and willing."

5- Then the Son said to the Father: "Your will with power, power with humility, humility with wisdom, wisdom with mercy. Let your will be done, which is and will be without beginning and without end in me! I take it to myself in my love, in your power and the rule of the Holy Spirit, who is not three gods but one God.

6- Then the Son said to his bride: "You have heard how the Father assigned you to me as an egg. You must therefore be simple and patient as an egg and fruitful to feed and clothe."

7- For there are three in the world. The first is completely naked, the second is cutting, and the third is hungry. The first signifies the faith of my Church, which is naked, because all are ashamed to speak of my faith and commandments. And if there are those who speak, they are reproached and accused of lying.

8- Therefore, my words, which proceed from my mouth, must clothe this faith as wool. For as wool grows in your body from heat, so from the heat of my divinity and humanity my words proceed to your heart, that they may clothe my holy faith with the testimony of truth and wisdom and prove it to be true, which is now considered empty, so that those who are still lukewarm had they clothed themselves with faith in works of charity, having heard the charity of my words, let them be converted and rekindled to speak confidently and to act boldly.

9- The second signifies my friends, who desire, as usual, to complete my honor, and are disturbed by my dishonor. These, hearing from the sweetness of my words, will be intoxicated with my greater love, and others with them, now dead, will be inflamed with my love, hearing what kind of grace I do with sinners.

10- The third signifies those who think thus in their heart: 'If we knew', they say, 'the will of God and how we could live and were well instructed in the good way, we would gladly do what we could.' These are as if hungry to know my way, and no one can satisfy them, because no one has shown them perfectly what they are to do. And if it is shown, no one lived according to them.

11- And therefore, the words appear to them as if they were dead, because no one lived according to them. Therefore, I myself will show them what to do, and I will satiate them with my sweetness. For the temporal things, which are seen and now desired by almost all, cannot satiate a man, but excite more and more a desire to complain.

12- But my words and charity will satiate men and fill them with abundant comfort.

13- Therefore, you, my bride, who are my hearers, take care to maintain patience and obedience! For you have become mine out of all righteousness. And therefore, you must follow my will.

14- But he who wishes to follow the will of another must have three things: first, one agreement with him, secondly, similar works, thirdly, to withdraw from his enemies. But who are my enemies but pride and all sins? Therefore, you must depart from these, if you wish to follow my will."

Chapter 39

How in Christ at the time of his death faith, hope, and charity were perfectible, and they are imperfectly in us poor people.

1- I had three at my death. At first faith, when I bent my knees and prayed, knowing that the Father would be able to deliver me from my passion. Second hope, when I was so constantly waiting and saying, 'Not as I want'. Thirdly, charity, when I said 'Thy will be done!'

2- I also had bodily distress from the natural fear of passion, when a sweat of blood issued from the body. Therefore, my friends should not panic and abandon themselves, when tribulation is pressing upon them, I will show them in myself that the weak flesh always shrinks from trouble.

3- But you may complain, how the sweat of blood came out of my body. Of course, just as the blood of a sick person dries up in all the veins and is consumed in the veins, so my blood was consumed by the natural pain of death.

4- Finally, the Father, wishing to show the way by which heaven would be opened and man who had been shut out might enter, gave me out of love to suffer, so that my body, consumed by passion, might be glorified in glory. For my humanity could not come to glory through justice without suffering, although I could have done it through the power of my divinity.

5- How, then, do they deserve to enter into my glory, who have little faith, vain hope, and no charity? Finally, if they had faith in eternal joy and a terrible punishment, they would desire nothing but me.

6- If they believed that I see and know all things and that I am powerful in all things and that I demand judgment about all things, the world would be despicable to them, and they would be more afraid to sin before me because of the fear of me than for men.

7- If they had a firm hope, then their whole mind and thought would be towards me. If they had divine charity, they would at least think in their hearts, what I have done for them, how much work I have done in preaching, how much pain in passion, how much charity I have had in death, namely that I wanted to die before leaving them.

8- But their faith is weak, and as if it hangs in them, threatening danger even more;

9- Their hope is vain, because they hope that sin will be forgiven without justice and the truth of the judgment. They believe that the kingdom of heaven is free. They desire my mercy without tempering justice.

10- Their love towards me is all cold, because they are never kind enough to complain about me, unless they are forced by tribulation. How can I be warmed with such, who have neither right faith, nor firm hope, nor fervent charity towards me?

11- Therefore, when they cried out to me and said 'Have mercy on me, God!', they do not deserve to be heard or to enter into my glory, because they do not want to follow their Lord to suffering, therefore they will not follow him to glory.

12- For no soldier can please his master and be accepted into his grace after his fall, unless he first shows him some humility for his contempt."

Chapter 40

The creator of the words puts forward to the bride three kind questions: the first about the servitude of the husband and the dominion of the wife, the second about the work of the husband and the consummation of the wife, the third about the contempt of the master and the honor of the servant.

1- I am your creator and master. Tell me three things that I want from you!

2- How does that house stand, where the wife dresses like a lady and her husband like a gentleman? Is it right?"

3- Then she answered within her conscience: "No, Lord, it is right."

4- And the Lord: "I am the Lord of all and the king of the angels. I have clothed myself in my sera, that is, my humanity, only for benefit and necessity.

5- For I asked for nothing in the world but only meager living and clothing. But you, who are my bride, you want to be like a lady, to have dignity and honor and to walk honorably.

6- For what good are all these things? Surely all is vain and all will be left. Indeed, man was not created for such superfluity, but for necessity by nature.

7- But pride found this superfluity, which is now regarded and loved as the law.

8- Secondly, tell me, is it proper for a man to work from morning till evening, and for his wife to consume in one hour all that has been collected?"

9- Then she answered: "It is not right, but the wife is bound to live and do according to the will of the husband."

10- And the Lord said: "I acted like a man who works from morning to evening. For I worked from my youth until my passion, showing the way to go to heaven by preaching and completing the work preached.

11- My wife, that is to say, the soul that ought to be mine as a wife, consumes all this labor, when she lived luxuriously, so that nothing I have done is of any use to her, nor do I find in her any virtue in which I can take pleasure in her.

12- Thirdly, tell me, in whatever house the master is despised and the servant is honored, is it not indecent and abominable?"

13- And she: "Truly, it is so." And the Lord: "I am the Lord of all. My house is clean and man should be my servant by right. But I, the Lord, am now despised in the world and man is honored. Therefore you, whom I have chosen, take care to do my will, because everything that they are in the world, they are nothing but some foam of the sea and some vain vision!"

Chapter 41

The words of the creator, in the presence of the heavenly host and the bride, how the same creator complains about five men, namely, the pope with his clergy and the evils of the laity and the Jews and the pagans and the help sent to his friends, by which all men are meant, and about the most cruel sentence brought against the enemies.

1- I am the creator of all things, I was begotten by the Father before Lucifer and inseparably in the Father and the Father in me and one Spirit in both. Therefore, there is one God, the Father, the Son, and the Holy Spirit, and not three gods.

2- I am the one who promised Abraham an eternal inheritance and brought my people out of Egypt through Moses. I am the same who spoke in the prophets.

3- The Father sent me in the womb of a virgin, not separating himself from me but remaining inseparably with me, so that man, departing from God, might return to God through my love.

4- And now, in the presence of my army, who see and know all things in me, yet because of the knowledge and instruction of that bridegroom standing by, who cannot perceive spiritual things except through corporeal things, I complain before you about these five men standing here, because they offend me in many ways.

5- For just as by the name of Israel I once understood in the law the whole Israelite people, so now by these five men I understand all the people in the world.

6- The first is the ruler of the Church and his clerics, the second is the evil laity, the third the Jews, the fourth the pagans, the fifth my friends.

REVELATIONS

7- But concerning thee, Jew, I receive all the Jews who are secretly Christians and serve me with sincere love and right faith and perfect work in secret.

8- As for you, heathen, I welcome all those who would willingly walk in the way of my commands, if they knew how and if they were instructed, who also do by work, as much as they know and are able. These will in no way be judged by you.

9- Now therefore I complain against you, head of my Church, who sit in my seat, which I handed over to Peter and his successors to sit in that triple dignity and authority: first, that they might have the power to bind souls and release them from sin, secondly, that they might open heaven to the penitent, thirdly, that they might close heaven to the cursing and reviling.

10- But you, who ought to release souls and present them to me, you are truly a killer of souls. For I appointed Peter the shepherd and keeper of my sheep.

11- But you are the scatterer and tearer of them, and you are worse than Lucifer. For he himself had a grudge against me, and he did not desire to kill anyone but me, so that he might rule for me.

12- But you are so much worse, that you not only kill me by removing me from you by your evil works, but you also kill souls by your bad example.

13- I redeemed souls with my blood and committed them to you as a faithful friend. But you are handing them over to the repeated enemy from whom I redeemed them.

14- You are more unjust than Pilate, who condemned no one to death but me. But you not only judge me as the master of no one and worthy of no good, but you also condemn innocent souls and let go of the guilty ones.

15- You are a friendless Judas, who sold me alone. But you are not only selling me, but also the souls of my elect for your filthy lucre and your vain name.

16- You are more abominable than the Jews. They crucified only my body. But you crucify and punish the souls of my elect, to whom your malice and transgression is bitterer than any sword.

17- And therefore, because you are like Lucifer, more unjust than Pilate, more friendly than Judas, more abominable to the Jews, therefore I justly complain about you."

18- But to the second, that is to the laity, the Lord said: "I created all things for your benefit. You consented to me and I to you. You gave me your faith and promised with your oath that you would serve me."

19- But now you have departed from me like a man, ignorant of his God. You consider my words as lies, my works as vanity. You call my will and my commandments too high.

20- You have become a violator of the promised faith. You broke your oath and left my name. You have separated yourself from the number of my saints and you have come to the number of demons and have become their partner.

21- It seems to you that no one is worthy of praise and honor but yourself. Everything that is mine and that you are bound to do to me is difficult for you, but what pleases you is easy.

22- That is why I rightfully complain about you, because you broke your faith, which you gave me in baptism and thereafter. Moreover, and for my love, which I have shown you by word and deed, you accuse me of lying. For my passion you call me foolish."

23- And to the third, that is to the Jews, he said: "I began my love with you, I chose you as my people, I brought you out of slavery, I gave you my law and brought you into the land which I promised to your fathers, I sent you prophets to comfort you."

24- Then I chose a virgin from among you, from whom I received humanity. And now I complain against you, that you still do not want to believe, saying: 'Christ has not yet come, but he is yet to come.'"

25- But to the fourth, that is to the gentile, the Lord said: "I created you and redeemed you as a Christian and did all good things for your sake. But you are like a mad man, because you do not know what you are doing, like a blind man, because you do not know where you are going."

26- For you worship the creature for the creator, falsity for the truth, and put your knee before your lower one. That is why I complain about you."

27- And to the fifth he said: "Come forward, friend, nearer!" And immediately he said to the heavenly host: "Dear friends, I have one friend, by whom I understand many.

28- He is like a man shut up among the wicked and taken captive harshly. If he speaks the truth, they themselves stone his mouth. If he does good, they throw a spear into his chest.

29- Behold, my friends and all the saints, how long shall I put up with them and how long shall I suffer such contempt?"

30- Saint John the Baptist answered: "You are like a most pure mirror. For in you, as if in a mirror, we see and know everything without words. You are incomparable sweetness, in which all good is sweet to us. You are like the sharpest sword, who judges on horseback."

31- Then the Lord answered him: "True, my friend, you speak the truth. For in me my elect see all good and all justice, and even evil spirits, although not in the light but in their consciousness."

32- For just as a man, placed in prison, who had previously learned letters, who, although he is in darkness, nevertheless knows by no means what he has learned, although he does not see, so the demons, although they do not see my justice in the light of my brightness, nevertheless know and see in his consciousness.

33- I am also like a sword that divides two. So I give to each one as he deserves."

34- Then, joining the Lord, he said to blessed Peter: "You are the founder of my faith and of my Church. Say, listening to my army, I will do justice to these five men!"

35- Peter answered: "Praise and honor be to you, Lord, for your love, which you do with your land! May you be blessed by all your army, because you make us see and know in you all that has been and will be!"

36- For in you we see and know all things. But this is true justice, that the first who sits in your seat and has the works of Lucifer, loses with contempt the seat in which he is presumed to sit, and is almost a partaker of Lucifer.

37- Of the second is justice, that he that departeth from thy faith, may descend to hell with his head below and his feet above, because he despised thee, who should have been his head, and loved himself.

38- Of the third is justice, that he may not see your face and be punished according to his malice and lust, because the treacherous do not deserve to see your vision.

39- Of the fourth is justice, that like a madman he should be shut up and put in dark places.

40- Of the fifth is justice, that help may be sent to him.

41- When they heard this, the Lord answered: "I swear by God the Father, whose voice John the Baptist heard in the Jordan, I swear by the body that John baptized in the Jordan, saw and trembled, I swear by the Spirit who appeared in the form of a dove in the Jordan, that I will do justice on these five."

42- Then, adding, the Lord said to the first man of the above-mentioned five: "The sword of my severity will enter your body, which will enter from the upper part of the head and will be so deeply and powerfully embedded that it will never be pulled out.

43- Your seat will sink like a heavy stone, which does not rest until it reaches the deepest depths.

44- Your fingers, that is, the assessors, will burn with sulphurous and unquenchable fire. Your arms, that is, vicars, which ought to be stretched out for the advancement of souls but are stretched out for the benefit of the world and honor, will be judged by the penalty with which David says: 'Let his children become orphans and his wife a widow, and strangers shall receive his substance.'

45- What is 'his wife' but a soul, which is left by the glory of heaven and will be a widow from God?

46- 'His sons', that is, the virtues they seemed to have, and my simple ones who were under them, will be separated from them and their dignity and goods will be given to others. And they themselves will inherit eternal confusion instead of dignity.

47- Then the ornaments of their heads will sink into the mire of hell, from which they will never rise, so that, just as here they rose above others through honor and pride, so they will sink so deeply into hell before others that it will be impossible for them to rise.

48- Their members, i.e. all their followers and clerical supporters, are cut off from them and separated like a wall to be destroyed, where no stone is left upon a stone, nor will cement adhere to the stones nor will mercy come upon them, because my charity will never warm them nor build them into an eternal abode in heaven, but without end they will be tormented with their heads broken from all good.

49- And to the second I say: Because you do not want to keep the faith you promised me and have no love for me, I will send to you an animal that proceeds from a rushing torrent and will swallow you up.

50- And as a torrent always descends to the lower parts, so that animal will lead you to the lower parts of hell. And just as it is impossible for you to go up against a rushing torrent, so it is difficult for you ever to rise from hell.

51- To the third I say: Because you, Jew, no longer want to believe that I have come, therefore, when I come to the second judgment, you will see me not in my glory but in your conscience, and you will prove that everything I had said was true.

52- Then there remains for you a punishment according to your merits.

53- To the fourth I say: Because you no longer care to believe and do not want to know, your darkness will shine for you and your heart will be enlightened, so that you will know that my judgments are true, and yet you will not come to the light.

54- To the fifth I say: I will do three things for you. First, I will fill you inside with my heat, and second, I will make your mouth harder than any stone and more stable, so that the stones thrown at you will return. Thirdly, I will equip you with my weapons so that no spear will harm you, but everything will soften before you like wax before the fire.

55- Therefore, strengthen and stand manfully! For as a soldier, who hopes for the help of his master in battle, fights as long as there is any liquid in him, so stand firm and fight, because the Lord your God will give you help that no one can resist.

56- And because you are few in number, I will honor you and multiply you.

57- Behold, my friends, you see and know this in me, and thus they stand before me. My words which have now been spoken will be fulfilled. But they will never enter my kingdom, as long as I am king, unless they reform themselves. For none will be given heaven except to those who humble themselves and repent."

58- Then the whole army answered: "Praise be to you, Lord God, who are without beginning and without end!"

Chapter 42

The Virgin's words of exhortation to her bride, how she ought to love her son above all things, and how all virtues and graces are included in the glorious Virgin.

1- The mother spoke: "I had three things by which I pleased my son: humility, so that no creature, neither angel nor man, was humbler than me; secondly, I had obedience, by which I endeavored to obey my son in everything; thirdly, I had great charity.

2- Therefore, I have been honored threefold by my son. For at first I was made more honorable than angels and men, so that there is no power in God that does not shine in me, although he is the source and creator of all things.

3- But I am his creature, to whom he granted his grace before all others.

4- Secondly, for obedience I obtained such power that no sinner is so impure, if he turns to me with a purpose of amendment and with a broken heart, that he will not have forgiveness.

5- Thirdly, for love, God draws near to me in this way, that he who sees God sees me, and he who sees me can see divinity and humanity in me as in a mirror and me in God.

6- For whoever sees God sees in him three persons, and whoever sees me sees as if there were three persons. For the deity enclosed me in himself with soul and body and filled me with all power, so that there is no power in God that does not shine in me, although God himself is the father and giver of all powers.

7- For just as two bodies joined together - whatever one receives, the other receives - so God did to me. For there is no sweetness that is not in me, just as someone who has a core and a part shares it with another.

8- My soul and body are purer than the sun and cleaner than the mirror. Hence, just as three persons would be seen in a mirror, if they were bright, so in my purity can be seen the Father and the Son and the Holy Spirit.

9- For I had a son in my womb with a deity. Now he himself appears in me with divinity and humanity as in a mirror, because I am glorified.

10- Therefore, bride of my son, try to follow my humility and love nothing but my son!

Chapter 43

The words of the Son to the bride, how a man ascends from a little good to perfect good and descends from a little evil to the highest punishment.

1- The son spoke: "Sometimes a great reward arises from a small good. The date tree has a wonderful smell and in its fruit is a stone. If it is planted in rich soil, it becomes fat and fruitful and grows into a large tree."

2- But if it is placed in dry ground, it dries up. That land is too dry for good, which delights in sin. In which if the seed of virtue is sown, it does not grow fat.

3- But fat is the land of the mind of him who knows sin and laments that he has sinned. In which, if a touchstone is placed, that is to say, the seediness of my judgment and my power is planted, it is rooted with three roots in the mind.

4- At first, he thought he could do nothing without my help. Therefore, he opens his mouth to ask me. Secondly, he begins to give even a little alms in my name. Thirdly, he withdraws himself from his business to attend to me.

5- Then he begins to abstain in fasting and in the renunciation of the will properly, and this is the body of the tree.

6- Afterwards the branches of charity grow, when he draws all whom he can to good.

7- Then the fruit grows, when he also teaches others, as far as he knows, and intends with all his devotion, how he can increase my honor. I like this kind of fruit very much.

REVELATIONS

8- Thus, he ascended from the little to the perfect. When it first takes root through modest devotion, the body grows through abstinence, the branches multiply through charity, the fruit grows fat through preaching.

9- In a similar way, through a small evil, a man descends to the highest curse and the highest punishment.

10- Do you know what is the heaviest burden of those who are growing? Certainly this is the child who comes to be born and cannot be born but dies inside the mother's bowels, and from this the mother also breaks up and dies, whom the father carries with the child to the grave and buries with putrefaction.

11- Thus the devil does to the soul. For the soul is vicious as the wife of the devil, whose will it follows in all things; which then he conceives from the devil, when sin pleases him and he rejoices in it.

12- For as a mother conceives and produces fruit from a small seed, which is nothing but decay, so also the soul, when it delights in sin, produces great fruit for the devil.

13- From this the members and the strength of the body are formed, when sin is added upon sin and daily increased. And so the mother swells with increasing sins, wanting to obey, but is unable, because, being consumed by nature in sin, life is considered tedious, and she would gladly sin more, but she cannot and is not permitted by God.

14- Then there is the fear that he cannot accomplish his will. Absent fortitude and cheerfulness. There is pain and anxiety everywhere.

15- Then the belly breaks, when he despairs of being able to do good. Then also he dies, when he blasphemes the judgment of God and reproves it, and is thus led by the devil his father to the grave of hell, where he is buried with the rottenness of sin and the son of pleasure without end.

16- Behold, how from a little sin increases and grows to damnation!"

Chapter 44

The words of the creator to the bride, how he is now despised and reproached by men, not paying attention to what he did out of charity by warning in the prophets and even himself by interceding for them, and not caring about his anger, which he exercised against the obstinate by cruelly correcting them.

1- I am the creator of all things and the Lord. I made the world and the world rejects me. I hear from the world the voice of a great bee that gathers honey on the earth.

2- For just as the greater bee, when it flies, immediately descends to the ground again and emits a very hoarse voice, so now in the world I hear that hoarse voice saying: 'I do not care what follows after this.' For all are already crying out: 'I don't care.'

3- Truly, man does not pay attention or care, what I have done out of charity by admonishing the prophets, by preaching through myself, by making peace for them. They do not care what I have done in my wrath by correcting the wicked and the disobedient.

4- They see themselves as mortal and uncertain about death and do not care. They hear and see my justice, which I exercised because of the sins of Pharaoh and the Sodomites, which I did to kings and other princes, which I allow to be done daily by the sword and other tribulations. And these things are as if blind to them.

5- Therefore, like the greater bees, they fly to whatever they want. For they sometimes fly as if by dancing, because they lift themselves up with their pride, but lower themselves more quickly when they return to their lust and gluttony.

6- They also gather sweetness, but for themselves and on earth, because man labors and gathers for the benefit of the body, not of the soul, and for earthly honor, not eternal.

7- They turn the temporal into a punishment for themselves, that which is of no use into an everlasting punishment. 8 Therefore, because of the prayers of my mother, I will send to these bees, from whom my friends are exempt, who are not in the world but in the body, my clear voice that will preach mercy; but if they hear, they shall be saved."

Chapter 45

The response of the Mother and the angels, prophets, apostles and demons to God, the bride present, testifying to his magnificence in creation and incarnation and redemption, etc., and how people now contradict all these, and about their judgment.

1- The mother said: "Dress yourself, my son's bride, and stand still, because my son is approaching you."

2- His flesh was pressed as in a press. For as a man transgresses in all his members, so my Son himself has satisfied in all.

3- The hair of my son was stretched out, the sinews were stretched, the joints were pulled from the frames, the bones were wavy, the hands and feet were fastened. The mind was troubled, the heart was afflicted with pain, the bowels contracted at the back, because man had sinned in all his members."

4- Then the son spoke, standing by the heavenly host, and said: "It is true that you know everything about me, yet I speak for the sake of this bride of mine who is standing.

5- I ask of you, angels: Tell me, what is this that was without beginning and will be without end? And what is this that created all things and was created by no one? Speak and bear witness!"

6- The angels answered as if with one voice, saying: "Lord, you are he. For we bear witness to you about three things:

7- First, that you are our creator and of all that are in heaven and on earth. Secondly, because you are without beginning and will be without end, your dominion and your power are eternal. For without you nothing has been done and without you nothing can be done.

8- Thirdly, we testify that we see in you all justice and all that has been and will be, and all things are in your foreknowledge without beginning and without end.

9- Then he said to the prophets and patriarchs: "I ask of you: Who brought you out of slavery into freedom? Who divided the water before you? Who gave you the law? Who gave you the spirit of speaking to the prophets?"

10- They answered him: "You, Lord. You brought us out of slavery. You gave the law. You raised our spirits to speak."

11- Then he said to his mother: "Give testimony of the truth that you know about me!"

12- She answered: "Before the angel sent by you came to me, I was alone with body and soul. But when the word of the angel was spoken, your body was in me with divinity and humanity, and I felt your body in my body."

13- I carried you without pain, I gave birth without distress. I wrapped you in clothes, fed you with my milk. I have been with you from birth to death."

14- Then the Lord said to the apostles: "Say, who is he whom you saw, heard and felt?"

15- They answered him: "We heard your words and wrote them down. We heard your great deeds, when you gave a new law, with a word you commanded demons and they came out, with a word you raised the dead and healed the sick.

REVELATIONS

16- We have seen you in a human body. We have seen your magnificence in divine glory with humanity. We saw you delivered to your enemies and hanged on a tree. We saw in you the most bitter passion and laid in the grave. We felt you when you rose again.

17- We pulled back your hair and your face. We have healed the places of your wounds and your limbs.

18- You ate with us and gave your talks. You are truly the son of God and the son of a virgin.

19- We felt it, when you ascended to the right hand of the Father with humanity, where you are without end."

20- Then God said to the unclean spirits: "It is true that you hide the truth in your conscience, yet I command you to tell who diminishes your power."

21- They answered him: "Just as thieves, unless their feet are trampled with hardwood, do not speak the truth, so neither do we, unless compelled by your divine and terrible power, would not speak the truth."

22- You are the one who descended to hell with your strength. You have diminished our power in the world. You have received your due from hell."

23- Then the Lord said: "Behold, all who have a spirit and are not clothed with a body bear witness to the truth to me. But those who have a spirit and a body, that is, men, contradict me. But some know but do not care. Others do not know. Therefore they do not care but say everything is false."

24- Again he said to the angels: "They say that your testimony is false, that I am not the creator and all things are known to me. Therefore they love the creature more than me."

25- And he said to the prophets: "They contradict you, saying that the law is vanity, that you were delivered by your strength and cunning, that the spirit was falsity, and that you spoke of your own will."

26- And he said to his mother: "Some say that you were not a virgin, others that I did not take the body from you, others know but do not care."

27- And he said to the apostles: "They contradict you, because they say that you are liars, a new law that is good for nothing and without reason. There are others who believe that it is true but do not care. Now therefore I ask you: Who will be their judge?"

28- They all answered him: "You, God, who are without beginning and without end. You, Jesus Christ, who are with the Father. Judgment has been given to you by the Father, you are the judge of these."

29- The Lord answered: "I, who complained against them, am now their judge, but even though I can and know all things, you still give your judgment over them!"

30- They answered him: "Just as the whole world in the beginning perished by the waters of the flood, so now the world is worthy to perish by fire, because now there is more iniquity and injustice than then."

31- The Lord answered: "Because I am just and merciful, and I do not judge without mercy, nor mercy without justice, therefore once more because of the prayers of my mother and my saints I will send my mercy to the world. But if they refuse to listen, justice will follow all the more severely."

Chapter 46

The words of praise of the Mother and of the Son together, the present bride, and how now Christ is considered and said by men to be dishonorable, most vile and base, and of the eternal damnation of such.

1- Mary spoke to her son, saying: "Blessed are you, who are without beginning and without end! You had the most honorable and decent body. You were the most energetic and virtuous man. You were the most worthy of creation."

2- The son answered: "Your words, which proceed from your mouth, are sweet to me and delight the innermost part of my heart like the sweetest drink. You are the sweetest to me of all creatures. For just as in a mirror different faces are considered but none pleases me more than my own, so I, although I love my saints, yet I love you with a special love, because I was begotten of your flesh.

3- You are like myrrh, the smell of which ascended to the deity and brought it into your body. This same smell drew your body and soul into the deity, where you are now with body and soul.

4- Blessed are you, because the angels rejoice because of your beauty and because of your power all who call on you with a sincere heart are delivered. In your light all the demons tremble and do not dare to stand before your light, because they always want to be in darkness.

5- Thou hast given me a threefold praise, because thou hast said that I have the most respectable body;

6- But those who have body and soul only contradict these tribes. For they say that I have a dishonorable body, that I am a most despised man, a most base creature.

7- What is more dishonest than to provoke others to sin? Thus they say that my body draws me to sin. For they say that sin is not so deformed as it is said, nor is it so much to displease God.

8- 'For', they say, 'nothing came into being unless God willed it, nor was anything created without Him. Why, then, should we not use these, which have been made, according to our will? The fragility of nature demands this, and so all before us have lived and live.'

9- This is how people talk to me now. But my humanity, in which I appeared as the true God among men, because I dissuaded sin and showed how great it is, they say dishonesty, as if I encouraged uselessness and dishonesty. For they say that nothing is honest but sin and what pleases their will.

10- They also say that I am a very ugly man. For what is worse than that? When he speaks the truth, his mouth is crushed with stones and his face is thrown, and he also hears the reproachful saying: 'If he were a man, he would avenge himself.' So they do to me.

11- I speak to them through the teachers and the Holy Scriptures, but they say that what I speak is a lie. They crush my mouth with stones and fists, when they commit adultery, murder, and lies, and say: 'If he were a man, if he were a mighty God, he would avenge such a transgression.'

12- But I suffer through my patience, and I hear them saying every day that the punishment is not eternal nor bitter, as it is said, and my words are judged to be a lie.

13- Thirdly, they judge me to be the lowest creature. For what is more abhorred in a house than a dog and a mouse, for which he who wished to commute would gladly receive a horse?

14- But man has me worse than a dog. For he would not receive me for this, that he might lose the dog; But what thing so small, alluding to the mind, is not thought and coveted more fervently than I? For if they esteemed me more than any other creature, they would love me more than others.

15- They have nothing so little that they do not love more than me. They grieve about everything beyond me. They grieve the loss of themselves and of their friends. They hurt one word. They grieve because they offend other men who are superior to themselves, but they do not grieve because they offend Me, the Creator of all.

16- What man is so repulsed, that if he asked, he would not be heard, and if he gave, nothing would be returned to him? But I am the most rejected and the most despicable in their sight, because they consider me worthy of no good, who gave them all good things.

17- Therefore, my mother, because you have tasted more of my wisdom and nothing but the truth has ever proceeded from your mouth, so nothing but the truth has ever proceeded from my mouth. I will excuse myself in the presence of all the saints before the first one who said that I have the most indecent body, and I will prove that I truly have the most decent body without deformity and sin, and he himself will come into eternal reproach, which everyone will see.

18- But he who called my words a lie and did not know whether I am God or not, I will prove that I am truly God, and he himself will fall down like mud into hell.

19- And the third, who judged me to be the most vile, I will judge him to eternal damnation, so that he may never see my glory and my joy."

20- Then he said to the bride: "Stand firmly in my service! You have come, as it were, to a kind of wall, in which you cannot escape nor dig the foundation.

Therefore, willingly suffer a little tribulation, and you will feel eternal rest in my arm!"

21- You know the will of the Father, you hear the words of the Son and feel my Spirit. You have pleasure and comfort in the address of my mother and my saints. So stand firm! Otherwise, you will feel my justice, by which you will be forced to do what I now kindly advise you to do."

Chapter 47

The Lord's words to the bride about the new addition of the law and how the law itself is now rejected and despised by the world and how evil priests are not God's priests but God's traitors and about the cursing and damnation of such.

1- I am that God who was once called the God of Abraham and the God of Isaac and the God of Jacob. I am God who gave the law to Moses. This was like a garment. For as a mother who has a child in her womb prepares clothes for the child, so God prepared the law, which was nothing but a garment and a shadow and a sign of things to come.

2- But I clothed myself and wrapped myself in these garments of the law. Then, just as a growing child changes the old habit and assumes a new one, I, having completed and laid aside the garment of the ancient law, took on a new garment, that is, the new law, and gave them to all who wanted to have garments with me.

3- But this garment is not tight or difficult, but everywhere moderate. For it does not command one to fast too much, or to work too much, or to kill oneself, or to do anything beyond possibility, but it is profitable for the control and chastisement of the soul and body.

4- For when the body adheres too much to sin, sin itself consumes the body.

5- In the new law, then, two things are found: first, discreet temperance and the right use of all things of soul and body; secondly, the ease of keeping the law, because he who cannot stand in one can stand in another.

6- It is found there that he who cannot be a virgin can lawfully be married. He who falls can rise again. But that law is now rejected and despised by the world.

7- For they say that the law itself is strict, gross and ugly. They say it is strict, because the law commands us to be content with what is necessary and to avoid what is superfluous. But they want to have everything out of proportion, like cattle over their physical strength. That is why it is strict for them.

8- They say that it is secondly important, because the law says to have pleasure with reason and at appointed times. But they themselves want to complete their pleasure more than is expedient and more than is appointed.

9- Thirdly, they say that it is ugly, because the law commands to love humility and to attribute all good things to God. But they want to be proud of the goods given by God and to exalt themselves. Therefore it is ugly to them. Behold, my garment is thus despised.

10- I completed all the previous ones and began new ones, because the old ones were too difficult to last until I came to judgment. But they cheaply threw away the garment with which the soul is covered, that is, right faith.

11- Moreover, they add sin to sin, because they want to betray me also. Does David say in the psalm: 'He who ate my bread thought to betray me'?

12- In those words I want you to note two things. First, that he does not say 'he thinks' but 'he thought', as if it were already in the past. Secondly, he notes that there was only one man who betrayed him.

13- But I say that they are my betrayers, who are in the present, not those who were or those who will be, but those who are already alive. I also say that it is not only one person but because there are many.

14- But perhaps you can complain of me: 'Are there not two kinds of bread, one invisible and spiritual, on which angels and saints live, the other from the earth, on which men are fed? But the angels and the saints will do nothing else but according to your will, and men can do nothing else but as it pleases you. How then can they betray you?'

15- I answer you, listening to my heavenly host, who knows and sees everything in me, but for your sake, so that you may know: There is truly twofold bread.

16- One of the angels who eat my bread in my kingdom, that they may be filled with my ineffable glory. For they do not betray me, because they want nothing else but like me.

17- But they betray me by eating my bread on the altar. I really am that bread. Three things are seen in that bread: shape, taste, and roundness.

18- I really am bread. For I, like bread, have three things in me, flavor, shape, and roundness. Taste, because, just as without bread all food is as insipid and as if without any strength, so without me everything, whatever it is, is tasteless and everything is weak and useless.

19- I also have the form of bread, because I am of the earth. For I am from a virgin mother, a mother from Adam, Adam from the earth.

20- I also have a roundness, where neither end nor beginning is found, because I am without beginning and without end. No one can consider or find an end or a beginning in my wisdom, power or charity. I am within all and above all and beyond all.

21- Even if someone were to fly like an arrow without ceasing forever, he would never find an end or depth in my power and strength.

22- Because of these three things, namely, flavor, shape, and roundness, I am that bread which is seen and felt on the altar of bread, but turns into my body, which was crucified.

23- For just as something dry and quickly burning, if it is stirred into fire, is quickly consumed and nothing remains of the shape of the wood but is all fire, so, when those words are said, namely, 'This is my body,' which before was bread, immediately becomes my body and not it is burned like wood by fire but by my deity. Therefore, those who eat my bread betray me.

24- But what can be a more abominable murder than that, where a man kills himself? Or what worse treachery than when two, united by an indissoluble bond, one betrays the other, as a married couple?

25- But what does a partner do when he wants to betray his partner? He really says to him under the pretense: 'Let us go to that place, so that I may fulfill my will with you!' And she, in true simplicity, ready to obey every will of her husband, goes with him.

26- But when he finds an opportune time and place, he produces against her three instruments of treachery. For either it has something so heavy that it kills it with a single blow, or something so sharp that it immediately enters the bowels, or something with which it is immediately suffocated and the vital breath is cut off.

27- But when she was dead, the traitor thought to himself: 'Now I have done wrong. If my deed be open and public, I shall be condemned to death.' Therefore he goes and places the body of his dead spouse in a secret place, so that his sin may not be discovered.

28- This is what my priests are doing now, who are my traitors. For they and I are bound together by one bond, when they take the bread and uttering words they make from it my true body, which I took from a virgin. Not all the angels can do this, because I gave that dignity only to the priests and chose them to the highest ranks.

29- But they themselves act like traitors to me. For they show me a happy and pleasant face, and lead me into a secret place, that they may betray me.

30- The priests themselves then show a happy countenance, when they appear to be good and simple, they lead me into the sanctuary, when they proceed to the altar. Then I was ready as a bride or groom to do all their will, but they betrayed me.

31- At first they apply to me a weighty one, when the divine duty, which they say to me, is burdensome and heavy to them. For a hundred words speak more for the world than one for my honor. They would rather give a hundred marks of gold for the world than a penny for me. They would work harder for their own benefit and the world than once for my honor. They weigh me down with this burden, as if I were dead from their hearts.

32- Secondly, they prick me as with a sharp knife which enters into the bowels, when the priest approaches the altar and thinks that he has sinned and repents, having a firm will to sin again after completing the office, thinking to himself: 'Well I repent of the sin, but I will not leave it from me, by which I have sinned, so that I will do it no more.' They stab me like a very sharp knife.

33- Thirdly, it is as if the spirit is suffocated, when they think to themselves thus: 'It is good and pleasant to be with the world, it is good to lust and I cannot restrain myself. I will do my will in my youth. But when I am old, then I want to abstain and improve myself.' And from this worst thought the spirit is suffocated.

34- But he complains, how. Of course, their hearts are so cold and warmed by me and by all that is good, that they can never be warmed or rise again to my love.

35- For just as from ice, even if fire is used, the flame does not arise but melts, so these, even if I give them my grace and they hear the words of warning, yet do not rise to the way of the vine but fall away and fail from all good.

36- Thus they betray me, namely, because they show themselves to be simple and are not, and because they are offended or disturbed by my honor, which they should be pleased with, and because they have a will to sin and because they promise that they will sin to the end.

37- Then I will act as if they hide me and put me in a secret place, when they think to themselves thus: 'I know that I have sinned. If I abstain from the sacrifice, I am confused and judged by all.' And they approach the altar shamelessly and place me before them and treat me as true God and man. With whom I am, as it were, in a secret place, because no one knows or considers how ugly and ugly they are, before whom I lie as if in a secret place, because, indeed, if the worst man were a priest and said those words, namely, 'This is my body,' he himself He consecrates my true body and I lie before him, true God and man.

38- But when he has applied me to his mouth, then I am taken down by grace with my divinity and humanity from him - but the form of the bread and the taste remain for him - not because I am not truly there with the bad as well as with the good because of the institution of the sacrament good and bad do not have the same effect.

39- Behold, such priests are not my priests, but traitors to the truth! For they also sell me like Judas and betray me. I see the Gentiles and the Jews, but I see none worse than them, because the priests themselves are in the same sin with which Lucifer fell.

40- Now I will also tell you their judgment and what they are like. The judgment of these is a curse. Just as David cursed those who do not obey God, - who, being a just prophet and king, did not curse out of anger or ill will or impatience but from the justice of God - so I, who am better than David, curse them who are priests. not from anger or ill will, but from justice.

41- Cursed therefore be all that they have received from the earth for their own use, because they do not praise God and their creator, who gave them this. Cursed be the food and drink of those who enter their mouths, who feed the body on the food of worms and the soul on hell.

42- Cursed be their bodies, which will rise again in hell to burn without end. Cursed be the years of those who have lived in vain. Cursed be the hour that begins for them in hell and will never end.

43- Cursed be the eyes of those who saw the light of heaven. Cursed be the ears of those who heard my words and did not care. Cursed be the taste of those who tasted my gifts.

44- Cursed be their touch with which they treated me. Cursed be their fragrance, with which they smelled of delights and neglected Me, the most delightful of all.

45- But he complains, how they are cursed. Of course their vision will be cursed, because they will not see the vision of God in themselves but the darkness and punishments of hell. Cursed are their ears, because they will not hear my words but the cry of hell and horror.

46- Their taste is cursed, because they will not taste of my eternal goods and joy, but eternal bitterness. Cursed is their touch, because they will not treat me but eternal fire. Cursed is their smell, because they will not smell that most sweet smell in my kingdom, surpassing all spices, but they will have a stench in hell more bitter than hide and worse than sulfur.

47- May they be cursed by earth and heaven and by all senseless creatures, because they obey God and praise him and they despise them.

48- Therefore, I swear in my truth, who am the truth, that if they die like this and in such a disposition, in which they are now established, my charity and virtue will never conclude them in themselves, but they will be damned without end."

Chapter 48

How, when the host of heaven and his bride are present, the deity speaks to humanity against the Christians, as the God of Moses against the people, and how the accursed priests love the world and despise Christ, and of their cursing and damnation.

1- A great army was seen in heaven, to which God said: "Look, my friends who are listening, who know and understand and see everything in me, I am speaking because of this bride of mine who is standing here."

2- Behold, as a man speaks to himself, so my deity speaks to my humanity. Moses was with the Lord on the mountain forty days and nights. When the people saw that he had been absent for so long, they took the gold and threw it into the fire, and thence was melted into a calf, which they called their god.

3- Then God said to Moses: 'The people have sinned. I will erase him, as something written is erased from a book.'

4- Moses answered: 'No, my Lord! Remember that you brought them out of the Red Sea and did wonderful things for them. If you destroy them, then where is your promise? Do not, I beg you, do this, because then your enemies will say: The God of Israel is evil, who brought the people out of the sea and killed them in the desert.' And God was appeased by these words.

5- I am that Moses in figure. My deity speaks to humanity, as if to Moses, saying: 'Look, what your people have done, how they have despised me! All Christians will be killed and their faith destroyed.'

6- My humanity answered: 'No, Lord. Remember that I brought the people across the sea in my blood, when I was torn from the sole of the foot to the top! I promised them eternal life. Have mercy on them because of my passion!'

7- After hearing these, the deity was appeased by these words and said: 'Thy will be done, because all judgment is given to thee! Behold, my friends, what kind of charity! But now before you, my spiritual friends, that is, angels and saints, and before my corporeal friends who are in the world, but who are not in the world but in the body, I complain that my people gathered wood and kindled a fire and threw gold into it. And then rose up to them a calf, whom they worship as a god.

8- He stands like a calf on four feet, having a head with a throat and a tail. And as Moses lingered on the mountain, the people said: 'We do not know what has happened to him.' And he displeased them because he had brought them out of captivity, saying: 'Let us ask another God to go before us!'

9- These accursed priests are doing this to me now. For they say: 'Why do we lead a more austere life than others?' or 'What is our reward? It is better for us to be at our own peace and pleasure. Let us therefore love the world, of which we are sure! For we are uncertain of his promise.'

10- Then they gather wood, that is, they apply all their senses to the love of the world. They kindle the fire when they have a perfect will to the world. But they burn when pleasure rages in the mind and betrays it in action. Afterwards they throw away the gold, that is to say, they do all the charity and honor which they ought to do to me, for the honor of the world.

11- Then arises the calf, that is, the complete love of the world, which has four feet, namely, gluttony, impatience, superfluous joy, and avarice. For the priests themselves, who ought to be mine, are eager to honor me, impatient to strike, excessive in joy, and never satisfied with what they wish.

12- This calf has both a head and a throat, that is to say, all the will to the mouth, so that it can never be satisfied, even if the whole sea overflows. But the tail of this calf is their malice, because they would not allow any of their own to possess it, if they could.

13- For they have offended and overthrown all those who serve me by their bad example and contempt. Such is the calf of love in their hearts. They rejoice and delight in such things.

14- They think of me, as they did of Moses: 'It has been long,' they say, 'missing.' His words seem vain and his works burdensome. Let us have our will, our power, and let God be our pleasure!'

15- Nor are they satisfied with these things, nor do they completely forget me, but have me as an idol.

16- Gentiles worshiped wood and stones and dead men. Among them was worshiped one idol named Beelzebub, whose priests offered incense to him and made kneelings and shouts of praise to him.

17- I will eat all that was useless of their sacrifice, it fell to the ground, and the fowls and flies ate it. But all that was useful, the priests reserved for themselves.

18- They also closed the gate over their idol and personally locked the door so that no one else could enter.

19- This is what the priests do to me at this time. They offer me incense, that is, they speak and preach beautiful words for their own praise and to have something temporal, not from my charity.

20- Therefore, just as the smell of incense is not perceived but is felt and seen, so their words do not come to the effect of souls, so that they can be rooted or held in the heart, but only the words are heard and seem to please for a time.

21- They offer prayers, but in no way appease me. Just as those who shout praise with their mouths and are silent with their hearts, they stand as if by my side crying with their mouths but wandering around the world with their hearts.

22- For if they had to speak to a man of some dignity, they should have a heart with their speech, lest they should hesitate in speaking, lest they should perhaps be noted in some.

23- But with me the priests pray like men who are in ecstasy, who speak one thing with their mouth and have another in their heart. Of whose words the hearer can have no certainty.

24- They bow their knees to me, that is, they promise me humility and obedience. But they are really humble like Lucifer. They are obeying their desires, not mine.

25- They also close on me and have a personal lock. Then they open upon me and praise me, when they say: 'Thy will be done as it is in heaven and on earth!'

26- But they close upon me when their will is accomplished; but mine is like that of a closed man and powerless, which can neither be seen nor heard.

27- Let them close the door personally, when I will draw back others who want to do my will by their example. And, if they could, they would also gladly prevent my will from going forth and being accomplished except according to their will.

28- Then they preserve in the sacrifice everything that is necessary and useful to them, and they demand all the honor and their due, but of the body of men, which falls to the earth by death, for which they were bound to offer the most important sacrifice, as if they judged it useless, handing it over to flies, that is to worms .

29- But they care little and pay no attention to his debt or to the safety of his soul.

30- But what was said to Moses? 'Kill those who made this idol!' Where if some were slain, yet not all. So now my words will come to kill them, some to body and soul through eternal damnation, others to life, that they may be converted and live, others to a quick death, because the priests themselves are absolutely hateful to me.

31- And to whom shall I liken them? They are truly like the fruit of a thorn, which is beautiful and red on the outside, but inside is full of filth and thorns. Thus he himself approaches me as men with ruddy love, and they appear clean to men, but inside they are full of all filthiness.

32- If this fruit is placed in the ground, other thorns will grow from it again. Thus they hide their sins and malice in their hearts, as if in the earth, and are so rooted in evil, that they are not even ashamed to come out and boast of their sin.

33- Wherefore others not only take the opportunity to sin, but are also seriously wounded to the soul, thinking to themselves thus: 'If the priests do this, it is much more lawful for us.'

34- For they themselves are not only like the fruit but also like the thorn, because they disdain to be touched by corrections and admonitions, and they consider no one wiser than themselves, but that they can do whatever they want.

35- Therefore I swear by my divinity and by the humanity of the angels who are listening, that I will break the door which they have closed against my will, and it will be fulfilled and their will will be annihilated and closed without end in punishment.

36- Therefore, as it was said of old, I will begin my judgment in the clergy and from my altar."

Chapter 49

Christ's words to the bride, how Christ himself is likened to Moses in figure, leading the people out of Egypt, and how the accursed priests, whom he chose as his greatest friends instead of the prophets, now cry: "Depart from us!"

1- The son spoke: "I likened myself first in the image of Moses. When he was leading the people, the water stood like a wall on the right and on the left."

2- I am certainly that Moses in figure, who led out the Christian people, that is, I opened heaven to them and showed them the way. But now I have chosen for myself other friends more special and more secret than the prophets, that is to say, the priests, who not only hear and see my words, when they see me myself, but even handle me with their hands, which none of the prophets or angels could do.

3- These priests, whom I have chosen as friends instead of prophets, do not cry to me with such longing and love as a prophet, but they cry with two contrary voices.

4- For they do not cry out like the prophet: 'Come, Lord, because you are sweet!', but they cry out: 'Depart from us, because your words are bitter and your works are grievous and cause us to stumble!'

5- Behold what the accursed priests say! I stand before them as the gentlest oui, from whom they take wool for clothing and milk for refreshment, and they still hate me for so much love.

6- I stand before them as a guest who says: 'Friend, give me the necessary life, because I need it, and receive the best reward from God!'

7- But they, because of your simplicity, drive me away like a wolf lying in wait for your father's family. Instead of hospitality, they confound me as a traitor unworthy of hospitality, and refuse to collect me.

8- But what is the rejected guest going to do? Should he produce arms against his domestic repulsor? No way. For this is not justice, because the possessor of his own can give and withhold his own to whom he wills.

9- So what is the guest going to do? Of course, he is bound to say to the repulsor: 'Friend, since you do not want to collect me, I will go to another who will show mercy to me.'

10- Who, coming to another, hears from him: 'You have come well, my lord, all that is mine is yours. You are now the master, but I want to be the servant and the guest.'

11- In such an inn, where I hear such a voice, I like to dwell. For I am like a guest rejected by men, but although I can enter everywhere by power, yet, by the dictates of justice, I do not enter except to those who, with good will, receive me as a true master, not as a guest, and who leave their will in my hands."

Chapter 50

The words of the Mother and the Son of blessing and praise and of the grace granted by the Son of the Mother for those existing in purgatory and remaining in this world.

1- Mary spoke to her son, saying: "Blessed be your name, my son, without end with your deity, which is without beginning and without end! In your deity there are three wonderful things, namely power, wisdom and virtue."

2- Your power is like a burning fire, before whose face everything that is firm and possible is counted as straw dried up in the fire.

3- Your wisdom is like the sea, which cannot be drawn in because of its greatness, because, when it rises and flows out, it covers valleys and mountains.

4- Thus your wisdom cannot be grasped and traced. How wisely you created man and set him over all your creation! How wisely you arranged the birds of the air, the beasts of the earth, the fish of the sea, and gave to each its time and order!

5- How wonderfully you give life to all and take it away! How wisely you give wisdom to the foolish and take it away from the proud!

6- Your power is like the light of the sun, which shines in the heavens and fills the earth with its light. So let your power satiate heaven and hell and fill all things. Therefore be thou blessed, my son, who art my God and my Lord!"

7- The son answered: "My dearest mother, your words are sweet to me, because they proceed from your soul. You are like the dawn proceeding with serenity.

8- Thou hast shone over all the heavens; Your light and your serenity surpassed all the angels. You drew to yourself with your serenity the true sun, that is, my divinity, to the extent that the sun of my divinity coming into you fixed itself in you, from whose heat you were warmed above all by my love, from whose brightness you were illuminated above all by my wisdom.

9- The darkness of the earth has been driven away and all the heavens have been illuminated by you.

10- I say in my truth that your purity, which pleased me above all the angels, drew my divinity into you, so that you were kindled by the heat of the Spirit, by which you enclosed the true God and man in your womb, by which man was enlightened and the angels rejoiced.

11- Therefore you are blessed by your blessed son! Therefore, there will be no request of yours to me that will not be heard, and through you all who ask for mercy with a desire to make amends will have grace. For as heat proceeds from the sun, so all mercy will be given through you. For you are like a well-flowing spring from which mercy flows to the poor."

12- The mother replied again to her son: "All power and glory be to you, my son! You are my God and mercy. From you is all the good that I have."

13- You are like a seed that was not sown and yet it grew and gave its one hundredth and thousandth fruit. For from you proceeds all mercy, which, because it is innumerable and indescribable, can well be signified in the hundredth number, in which perfection is marked, because from you is all perfect and perfection."

14- The son answered the mother: "Truly, mother, you have likened me to a seed, which was not sown and yet grew, because I came into you with divinity and my humanity was not sown from a mixture and yet grew in you, from which mercy flowed to all. That is why you said, " Now then, since you draw mercy from me with the sweetest words of your mouth, ask whatever you want, and it will be given to you."

15- The mother answered: "My son, because I have obtained mercy from you, therefore I ask for mercy and help for the poor. For there are four places. The first is heaven, in which the angels and the saints need no soul but you, whom they have. For they have in you everything good.

16- The second place is hell, and those who dwell therein are filled with malice and excluded from all mercy. Therefore nothing can enter them any more from good.

17- The third place is to be cleansed. For they are in need of threefold mercy, because they are afflicted threefold. For they are disturbed by the hearing, because they hear nothing else but near pains and misery.

18- They are distressed by the sight, because they see nothing but their own misery.

19- They are afflicted by the touch, because they feel the heat of the fire almost unbearable and high. Give them, my Lord and my son, your mercy because of my prayers!"

20- The son answered: "I will gladly give them threefold mercy for your sake. First, their hearing will be eased, their sight will be softened, their punishment will be milder and milder."

21- In addition, those who from that hour are in the highest punishment of purgatory will come to the middle. And those who are in the middle will come under the lightest penalty. But those who are in the lightest punishment will pass to rest."

22- The mother answered: "Praise and honor be to you, my Lord!" And immediately the mother added to her son: "The fourth place is the world, and its inhabitants need three: first, contrition for sins, second, satisfaction, third, strength to do good."

23- The son answered: "Everyone who calls on your name and has hope in you committed to the purpose of making amends, these three things will be given to him, in addition to the kingdom of heaven. For there is so much sweetness in your words to me that I cannot deny what you ask, because nothing You want something else but what I want.

24- In short, you are like a bright and burning flame, with which luminaries are kindled when they are extinguished, and when they are not kindled, they are kindled. But from your love, which ascended into my heart and drew me to you, let those who are dead in sins revive, and warm, like black smoke, they will be convalesce in my love."

Chapter 51

The words of the Mother's blessing to the Son, hearing the bride, and how the glorious Son represents most beautifully his sweetest mother through a flower, born in a valley, etc.

1- The mother spoke to her son, saying: "Blessed be your name, my son Jesus Christ! Honor be to your humanity above all that has been created! Glory be to your deity above the good omens, who with your humanity is one God."

2- The son answered: "My mother, you are like a flower that grew in one valley. Around which valley there were five high mountains. And the flower itself grew from three roots with a straight stem, which had no nodes.

3- This flower had five leaves, full of all sweetness. And the valley grew with its flower over these five mountains, and the leaves of the flower spread themselves over the whole height of heaven and over all the choirs of angels.

4- You, my beloved mother, are of that valley because of your humility, which you had before others. He went over five mountains.

5- The first mountain was Moses because of power. For he had power over my people in the law, as if he had been locked in his fist. But thou hast enclosed the lord of all laws in thy womb. That is why you are raised on that mountain.

6- The second mountain was Helias, who was so holy that he was taken up with soul and body into the holy place. As for you, my dearest mother, your soul was taken up above all the choirs of angels to the throne of God, and with it is your most pure body. That is why I call you Helia.

7- The third mountain was the strength of Sampson, which he had over all men. However, the devil overcame him with his deceptions. But you overcame the devil with your strength. That is why you are stronger than Sampson.

8- The fourth mountain was David, who was a man according to my heart and my will and yet fell into sin. But you, my mother, followed all my will and never sinned.

9- The fifth mountain was Solomon, who was full of wisdom. However, he was infatuated. But you, my mother, were full of all wisdom and were never foolish or deceived. Therefore, I am drawn to Solomon.

10- And the flower came forth from three roots, because you had three things from your youth, namely obedience, charity and divine intelligence.

11- For from these three roots grew the straightest shaft without any knot, that is, your will, which was never bent except to my will.

12- For this flower had five leaves, which grew over all the choirs of angels. Truly you, my mother, are the flower of these five leaves.

13- The first leaf is your honesty in so far as my angels, who are honest before me, considering your honesty, saw that it was above them and more eminent than them in sanctity and honesty. That is why you are more attractive than the angels.

14- The second leaf is your mercy, which was so great that when you saw the misery of all souls, you had compassion on them and suffered the penalty in my death.

15- Angels are full of mercy. Yet they never put up with pain, but you, most pious mother, were merciful to the poor, when you felt all the pain of my death, and out of mercy you wished to suffer pain rather than to be exempt from it. Therefore, your mercy exceeded the mercy of all angels.

16- The third leaf is your kindness. For angels are gentle and desire good for all, but you, my dearest mother, before your death had in your soul and body the will of an angel and did good to all. And you still deny it to anyone who reasonably asks for his benefit. And therefore, your kindness is more excellent than the angels.

17- The fourth leaf is your beauty. For the angels consider one another's beauty and marvel at the beauty of all souls and all bodies, but they see that the beauty of your soul is above all that has been created, and that the dignity of your body excels all men that have been created. And so thy beauty surpassed all the angels and all that was created.

18- The fifth leaf was your divine delight, because nothing pleased you but God. Thus, the angels are pleased with nothing but God, and each one of them feels and feels his delight in himself. But when they saw your delight in you towards God, it seemed to them in their consciousness that their delight burned in them like a light in divine love.

19- Seeing that your delight was like a burning pyre, burning with a most fervent fire and so high that its flame approached my deity. And therefore, sweetest mother, your divine delight burned well above all the choirs of angels.

20- This flower, which had these five leaves, that is, honesty and mercy, gentleness and beauty and supreme delight, was full of all sweetness.

21- But whoever wishes to taste sweetness must draw near to sweetness and receive it within himself. And so you did, good mother. For thou wast so sweet to my father, that he received thee whole into his spirit, and thy sweetness above all pleased him.

22- The flower also bears seed from the heat and power of the sun, from which the fruit grows. But blessed is that sun, namely my deity, who received humanity from your virgin entrails! For as a seed, wherever it is sown, sprouts such flowers as the seed was, so my members were conformed to your members in form and face. Yet I was a man and you a virgin woman.

23- This valley was exalted above all the mountains with its flower, when your body was exalted above all the choirs of angels with your most holy soul."

Chapter 52

The Mother's words of benediction and request to her Son, that her words may spread throughout the world and take root in the hearts of her friends, and how the Virgin herself is wonderfully depicted by the flower, born in the spring. And concerning the words of Christ, transmitted through the bride to the pope and to other prelates of the Church.

1- The blessed virgin spoke to her son, saying: "Blessed are you, my son and my God and lord of angels and king of glory! I beg you that your words which you have spoken may take root in the hearts of your friends and so firmly adhere to their minds as tar with which an ark Noah was anointed, which neither tempest nor wind could dissolve.

2- Let them also be spread throughout the world like the sweetest branches and flowers, the fragrance of which is spread far and wide. Moreover, let them bear fruit and be sweet like the date tree, whose sweetness delights the soul too much."

3- The son answered: "Blessed are you, my dearest mother! Gabriel, my angel, said to you: 'Blessed are you,' he said, 'be you, Mary, first of women!' And I give you testimony that you are blessed and most holy above all the choirs of angels.

4- Thou art like a flower in the spring, which, though many fragrant flowers surround it, nevertheless excels them all in fragrance, in beauty, and in virtue.

5- These flowers are all chosen from Adam until the end of the world. Those who, planted in the spring of the world, strove and flourished in various virtues, but among all those who have been and those who will come after, you were the most excellent in the fragrance of good life and humility, in the beauty of the most pleasing virginity, in the virtue of abstinence.

6- For I bear witness to you, that in my passion you were more than a martyr, in your abstinence more than any of the confessors, in mercy and good will more than an angel.

7- Therefore, because of you, I will root my words like the strongest bitumen in the hearts of my friends. They will expand like fragrant flowers and bear fruit like the most tender and sweet date tree."

8- Then the Lord spoke to the bride: "Tell your friend, as his father, whose heart is according to my heart, that he should explain these written words carefully, and he himself will assign them to the archbishop and afterwards to another bishop. After they have been carefully informed, he will later pass them on to the third bishop."

9- To say to him from my side: 'I am your creator and redeemer of souls. I am the God whom you love and love above all others. Consider and see that the souls which I have redeemed with my blood are like the souls of those who do not know God and are held captive by the devil so terribly that he punishes them in all their members as if in a tight press.

10- Therefore, if my wounds are good in your heart, if you have my scourging and the pain of some reputation, show by your works how much you love me!

11- And make my words, which I have spoken with my own mouth, come to the public, and bring them personally to the head of the Church! For I will give you my spirit, so that wherever there is a disagreement between two, you can confederate in my name by the power given to you, if they believe.

12- Moreover, and for the greater evidence of my words, you shall bring with you to the pontiff the testimonies of those to whom my words are wise and pleasing.

13- For my words are like wax, which, the greater the heat within, the more quickly it melts. But where there is no heat, it is rejected and does not reach the interior.

14- These are my words, because the more a man, fervent with my love, eats and wears them, the more he is affected by the sweetness of heavenly longing and internal love, and the more he burns for my love.

15- But those who do not like my words are as if they have a sore in their mouth. When they have tasted it, they immediately throw it out of their mouths and trample it underfoot. Thus, my words are despised by some, because they do not like the sweetness of spiritual things.

16- And the prince of the earth, whom I have chosen as my member and made truly mine, will manfully help you and provide you with the necessary services for the way out of your well-acquired goods.'

Chapter 53

The words of the Mother and the Son of blessing and praise are united, and how the Virgin is represented by the ark, where were the rod, the manna, and the tablet of the law, in which many wonderful things are contained.

1- Mary spoke to her son: "Blessed are you, my son, my God and Lord of the angels! You are the one whose voice the prophets heard, whose body the apostles saw, whom the Jews and your enemies felt.

2- You are one God with divinity and humanity and the Holy Spirit. For the prophets heard the Spirit, the apostles saw the glory of God, the Jews crucified your humanity. Therefore, may you be blessed without beginning and without end!"

3- The son answered: "Blessed are you, because you are a virgin and a mother! You are that ark that was in the law, in which there were three things, namely the rod, the manna and the tablet."

4- When the staff became three. At first she was changed into a serpent, which was without poison. Secondly, the sea was divided by it. A third water was drawn from the rock.

5- I am that rod in shape, which I laid in your belly and received humanity from you. I, in the first place, like the serpent of Moses, so I am terrible to my enemies. For he himself flees from me as from the sight of a serpent.

6- I am content to be held by them, if they will, I will return to them if they ask me. I run to them like a mother to a lost and found child, if they call me. I show them my mercy and forgive their sins if they cry out. I do this to them, and they still hate me like a snake.

7- Secondly, by means of that rod the sea was divided, when the way to heaven, which was closed by sin, was opened by my blood and pain. Then surely the sea broke, and the way was broken, when the pain of all my limbs came to the heart, and the heart was broken by the violence of the pain.

8- Afterwards, when the people had been brought across the sea, Moses did not immediately lead them into the land of promise, but into the desert, that they might be tested and trained there.

9- Thus and now, having accepted my faith and my command, the people are not immediately introduced into heaven, but it is necessary that in the wilderness, that is, in the world, men should be tested as to how they love God.

10- But in three ways the people provoked God in the wilderness. First, because they made an idol for themselves and worshiped it. Secondly, because they lusted after the flesh which they had in Egypt. Thirdly, through pride, when they wanted to go up without the will of God and fight with their enemies.

11- Even now man sins against me in the world. First he worships an idol, because he loves the world and those in it more than I, who am their creator.

12- But the world is their god, not I. For I said in my Gospel: 'Where a man's treasure is, there is his heart.' Thus the world is a man's treasure, because he has his heart for this, not for me.

13- Therefore, just as those in the desert fell by the sword in the body, so they will fall by the sword of eternal damnation to the soul, in which they will live without end.

14- Secondly, they sinned through the lust of the flesh. For I have given man all that is necessary for honesty and moderation, but he wants to have everything immoderately and indiscriminately.

15- For he himself, if nature were sufficient, would desire to mingle without ceasing, to drink without restraint, to lust without restraint. For as long as he could sin, he would never cease from sin.

16- Therefore it will happen to them, as it happened to them in the desert, that they will die a sudden death. For what is the life of that time but as a sort of point towards eternity? Therefore, as if by a sudden death, they will die in the body because of the brevity of this life, and live in endless punishment to the soul.

17- Thirdly, they sinned in the desert through pride, because they wanted to go up to battle without the will of God. Thus men, through their pride, want to ascend to heaven, and do not trust in me, but in themselves, doing their own will and forsaking mine.

18- Therefore, just as they were killed by their enemies, so they will be killed by demons in their souls, and their torment will be eternal. So then they hate me like a serpent, they worship an idol instead of me, they affect their concupiscence more than me, they love their pride instead of my humility.

19- Nevertheless, I am still so merciful that if they turn to me with a broken heart, I turn to them like a pious father and receive them.

20- Thirdly, by means of a rod, this rock gave water. This rock is the heart of a hard man. For this, if he is struck by my fear and love, they immediately flow with tears of contrition and penitence.

21- No one so unworthy, no one so bad, if he turns himself to me, if he considers my passion intimately, if he pays attention to my power, if he evaluates my goodness, how the earth produces fruit and the trees, that his lips do not flow with tears and all his limbs to devotion they are excited

REVELATIONS

22- Secondly, in the ark of Moses lay manna. Thus in thee, my mother and virgin, was laid the bread of the angels and holy souls and the righteous on earth, to whom nothing pleases but my sweetness, to whom the whole world is dead, who would gladly, if it were of my will, be without bodily food.

23- Thirdly, in that ark were the tablets of the law. Thus the lord of all laws rested upon you. Therefore, blessed are you above all that are created in heaven and on earth!"

24- Afterwards he spoke to his bride, saying: "Say three things to my friends! I, when I was conversing bodily in the world, so moderated my words, that the good ones became stronger and more fervent from them. But the bad ones became better, as was evident in Magdalene, Matthew and many others.

25- I also moderated my words so that my enemies could not weaken them. Therefore, let those to whom my words are sent work fervently, so that the good from my words may become more ardent in good, the evil may repent from evil, and beware of my enemies, lest my words be hindered.

26- For I do no greater wrong to the devil than to the angels in heaven. For if I wished, I could well speak my words for the whole world to hear.

27- It would be sufficient for me to open hell, so that all might see its punishments, but this would not be justice, because then man would serve me out of fear, but man should serve me out of charity. For no one but he who has charity will enter the kingdom of heaven.

28- Then, in short, I would be wronging the devil if I were to receive from him the freedom of his rights without good works. I would do wrong even to an angel in heaven, if the spirit of an unclean man should associate with him, who is pure and most ardent in charity.

29- Therefore no one will enter heaven unless he has been tested like gold in the fire of purgatory or has been trained in good works by such a long trial in the world, that there is no spot in him that needs to be cleansed.

30- If you do not know to whom my words should be sent, I will tell you. He is worthy to have my words, who wants to be earned by works, in order to come to the kingdom of heaven, or who has earned by previous good works; My words will be opened to them and they will enter into them.

31- For those to whom my words are wise and who humbly hope to have their name written in the book of the vine, these hold my words. But those who are not wise, indeed consider the words and immediately throw them away and leave them."

Chapter 54

The words of the angel to the bride about the spirit of his thoughts, whether it is good or bad, and how there are two spirits, one uncreated and the other created, and about their qualities.

1- The angel spoke to the bride saying: "There are two spirits, one uncreated, the other created. The uncreated has three. The first is hot, the second is sweet, the third is clean.

2- First, he warms, not from any created things, but from himself, because he, together with the Father and the Son, is the creator of all things and all-powerful. But it warms when the whole soul burns with the love of God.

3- Secondly, it is sweet, when nothing pleases the soul, nothing sweetens but God and the remembrance of his works.

4- The third is the world, so that no sin can be found in it, nothing deformed, nothing corruptible and changeable. But it heats not like a material fire or like the visible sun melting something, but its heat is the inner love of the soul and desire, filling and absorbing the soul into God.

5- The soul is also sweet, not like desirable wine or pleasure or anything else worldly, but that sweetness of the spirit is incomparable to all temporal sweetness and inexhaustible to those who are not wise.

6- Thirdly, that spirit is as pure as the rays of the sun, in which no spot can be found.

7- The second spirit, which is created, has three things in a similar manner. For it is burning, it is bitter, and it is unclean.

8- First, it is burning and consuming like a fire, because it burns the whole soul it possesses with the fire of lust and greed, so that the soul can think of nothing else beyond its satisfaction, and desire nothing, so much so that sometimes temporal life and all honor and consolation are lost because of it.

9- Secondly, it is bitter as gall, because it so inflames the soul with its pleasure, that future joys seem to it to be nil, and good eternal foolishness. All things, too, which are of God and which he is bound to do, are bitter to him and are abhorrent to him like vomit and like gall.

10- Thirdly, it is unclean, because it makes the soul so vile and prone to sin, that it would be ashamed of any sin and desist from any sin, if it did not fear the shame of men more than of God.

11- And that is why that spirit is burning like fire, because it burns for iniquity and sets others on fire with it. For that reason, he is bitter, because all good is bitter to himself, and he wants others to be bitter with him. And therefore, he is unclean, because he himself delights in uncleanness, and complains of having others like him with him.

12- But now you can complain and say to me: 'Are you not also a created spirit like him? Why then are you not like that?'

13- I answer you: I was truly created by the same God as myself, because there is only one God, the Father and the Son and the Holy Spirit, and these are not three gods, but one God. And we were both created well and for good, because God created nothing but good.

14- But I am like a star, because I stood in the goodness and love of God, in whom I was created. But he is like coal, because he departed from the love of God.

15- Therefore, just as a star is not without brightness and brightness, nor a coal without blackness, so a good angel, who is like a star, is not without brightness, that is, the Holy Spirit.

16- For everything that he has, he has from God, that is, the Father and the Son and the Holy Spirit. He is warmed by his love, he shines with his brightness, and he constantly clings to him and conforms to his will, and never wants anything else but what God wants. That's why it burns, that's why it's clean.

17- Now the devil is ugly like coal, and the ugliest of all creatures, because just as he was more beautiful than the others, so he should become uglier than others, because he opposed his creator.

18- But just as the angel of God shines with the light of God and burns unceasingly with his love, so the demon is always inflamed and distressed by his malice. His malice is insatiable, so is the goodness of the Holy Spirit and his grace indescribable. For there is no one in the world so rooted with the devil, whose heart is not sometimes visited and moved by a good spirit; so also there is no one so good whom the devil does not willingly touch with temptation.

19- For many good and righteous people are tempted by the devil by God's permission. This is not for their evil, but for their greater glory.

20- For the Son of God, one in deity with the Father and the Holy Spirit, was tempted in his assumed humanity. How much more his elect to their greater reward!

21- Even many good people sometimes fall into sins and their consciousness is overshadowed by the deceptions of the devil, but by the power of the Holy Spirit they rise stronger and stand stronger.

22- However, there is no one who does not understand in his conscience whether the suggestion of the devil leads to the deformity of sin or to good, if he is willing to think carefully and examine it.

23- Therefore, you, the bride of my Lord, do not have to doubt the spirit of your thoughts, whether it is good or bad. For your conscience tells you what to omit and what to choose.

24- But what will he do, with whom the devil is full? For a good spirit cannot enter him, because he is full of evil. There are three things that he must do, namely, that he should have a pure and complete confession of sins, which, although he cannot be immediately in a broken heart because of a hardened heart, yet it is only useful that because of this the devil gives, as it were, a kind of cessation and leap to the good spirit.

25- Secondly, let him have humility, namely, that he proposes to make amends for the sins he has committed, and to do the good he can, and then the devil begins to come out.

26- Thirdly, in order to obtain a good spirit again, he must supplicate God with a humble prayer and repent of the sins he has committed with true love, because love for God kills the devil.

27- In short, he himself would rather die in vain, than that a man should present the least good of charity to his God. He is so spiteful and malicious."

28- Afterwards the blessed Virgin spoke to her bride, saying: "My son's new bride, put on your clothes, put on your necklace, that is, the passion of my son!"

29- To whom she answered: "Put it on, my lady!" And she said: "I will certainly do it. I want to tell you how my son was disposed of and why he was so fervently desired by his fathers."

30- He stood as a man in the middle of the gap between two cities, and a voice from the first city called out to him, saying: 'You man, who stands in the middle of the road between the cities, you are a wise man. For you know to beware of impending dangers.

31- You, too, are strong enough to put up with bad incumbency. You are also magnanimous, because you fear nothing. For we longed for you and waited for you.

32- Then open our gate! For the enemies besiege it, that it may not be opened.'

33- A voice was heard from the second city saying: 'You, the most humane and most powerful man, hear our complaint and groan! We sit in darkness and suffer unbearable hunger and thirst.

34- Consider then our misery and pitiable poverty! For we have been smitten like hay cut by a scythe. We are cut off from every good thing and all our strength has failed.

35- Come to us and save us, because we waited for you alone, we hoped for you as our deliverer! Come and relieve our poverty, turn our mourning into joy! Be thou our help and salvation! I have come, O most worthy and blessed body, which proceeded from a pure virgin!'

36- My son heard these two voices from two cities, namely heaven and hell. Therefore, in mercy, through his most bitter passion and the shedding of his own blood, he opened the gates of hell and rescued his friends. He opened the heavens and brought in the gladdened angels who had been rescued from hell.

37- This, my daughter, think and always keep in mind!

Chapter 55

How Christ is likened to a mighty lord, building a great city and an excellent palace, by which the world and the Church are designated, and how the judges and defenders and laborers in the Church of God are gathered together in the bow of the bow.

1- I am like a powerful lord who, building a city, imposed on it a name from his own name. Then he built a palace in the city, in which there were various small rooms for the capture of necessaries. Having built the palace and arranged his affairs, he arranged his people into three parts, saying:

2- 'My ways are to remote parts. Stand and work manfully for my honor! For I have prepared for you your necessaries and victuals. You also have judges who will judge you. You have defenders who protect you from your enemies.

3- I have also appointed laborers who will feed you and will pay me a tenth part of their labor and reserve it for my benefit and honor.'

4- But after the intermission for some time the name of the city was forgotten. Then the judges said: 'Our Lord has gone to distant parts. Let us judge the right judgment and do justice, so that when we return to our master we will not be blamed but we will bring back honor and blessing.'

5- Then the defenders said: 'Our Lord trusts in us and has left us the custody of his house. Let us therefore abstain from excess food and drink, lest we be unfit for battle! Let us also refrain from excessive sleep, lest we be deceived by the unwary! Let us be well armed and constantly watchful, lest we be found unprepared by the coming enemies!

6- For the honor of our Lord and the safety of his people depend most upon us.

7- Then the workers also said: 'Great is the glory of our Lord and his glorious reward. Let us therefore work hard and give him not only a tenth part of our labor but also, whatever is left over from our subsistence, let us offer him! For the reward will be so much more glorious, as he sees our greater charity.'

8- After this proceeding, the lord of the city and the palace was again forgotten for a time. Then the judges said to themselves: 'The delay of our master is long, and we do not know whether he will return or not. Let us then judge according to our will, and let us do what pleases us!'

9- Then the defenders said: 'We are foolish, because we work and do not know for what reward. We would rather confide in our enemies, sleep and drink with them! For we have no need to worry about those who have been his enemies.'

10- Afterwards the workers said: 'Why should we keep our gold for another? And we do not know who will carry it back after us. It is better, therefore, that we use it by arranging ourselves to our will.

11- For we will give a tenth part to the judges, and having appeased them we can do what we want.'

12- I am truly like that mighty lord, who built for myself a city, that is, the world, in which I established a palace, that is, the Church. The name of the world was divine wisdom, because from the beginning the world had this name, which was made in divine wisdom.

13- This name was revered by all, and God was praised by his creation in his wisdom and was wonderfully preached. But now the name of citizenship has been dishonored and changed, and a new name has come, that is, human wisdom.

14- For the judges, who formerly judged in justice and in the fear of the Lord, are now turned to pride and supplant simple men. They desire to be eloquent, that they may have the praise of men; they speak pleasingly, that they may obtain favors.

15- They speak words lightly, that they may be called good and gentle; they receive gifts, that they may pervert judgment. They are wise for their temporal advantage and their own will, but dumb for my praise.

16- They trample the simple underfoot and make them dumb. They spread their greed to all and make falsehood out of what is right. This wisdom is now loved, but mine has been given over to oblivion.

17- But the defenders of the Church, who are courtiers and soldiers, see my enemies and the assailants of my Church and hide themselves. They hear their words of abuse and do not care.

18- They understand and feel the works of my commandments, and yet they bear them patiently. They look upon them every day lawfully committing all mortal sins, and do not repent, but sleep and converse with them, and bind themselves by oath to their company.

19- But the laborers, who are the whole community, reject my commandments and withhold my gifts and my tithes. They offer gifts to their judges and pay homage to them, so that they may find them lovable and agreeable.

20- I can truly boldly say that the sword of my fear and of my Church has been thrown away in the world and a bag of money has been taken for it.

Chapter 56

The words of how God declares the chapter immediately above, and of the judgment brought against such, and how God for a time supports evil for the sake of the good.

1- I went to you before because the sword of the Church was thrown away and a bag of money was taken for it, which is open on one side and so deep on the other that, whatever enters, it never reaches the bottom and is never filled.

2- This sack is covetousness, which exceeds all measure and measure, and has spread to such an extent that, in contempt of the Lord, nothing is desired but money and one's own will.

3- However, I am like a lord who is both father and judge. When he went to judge, the bystanders said: 'Lord, go quickly and judge!' The master answered them: 'Wait a little until tomorrow, because perhaps my son will improve himself in the meantime.'

4- And when he came the next day, the people said to him: 'Proceed and make judgments, sir! How long do you prolong judgment and not judge the guilty?'

5- The master replied: 'Wait a little longer, if my son will redeem himself! And then, if he does not come to his senses, I will do what is right.'

6- Thus I patiently suffer man to the very last point, because I am both father and judge. However, because my justice is unchangeable and however long it is prolonged, I will either punish the sinners if they have not reformed themselves, or I will show mercy to those who have repented.

7- I told you before that I divided the people into three parts, that is, into judges, defenders, and laborers. For what do these judges mean but clerics, who have turned the divine wisdom into profane and vain wisdom?

8- Just as those clerics are wont to do, who receive many words and combine them into a few - and those few words sound the same as those many - so the clerics of this time have received my ten commandments and combined them into one word.

9- What is this one word? 'Stretch out your hand and give me the money!' This is their wisdom, to speak well and act badly, to pretend to be mine and act wickedly against me.

10- In short, those who sin in exchange for their gifts willingly reconcile themselves to their sins and bring down the simple by their example. Besides, they hate those who walk my way.

11- Secondly, the defenders of the Church, that is, the courtiers, are infidels. Those who have broken their promise and oath and are sinning against the faith of my holy Church and the constitution willingly tolerate it.

12- Thirdly, the workers, that is, the community, are like untamed bulls, because they have three. For they dig up the earth with their feet, secondly they fill themselves to satiety, thirdly they fill their pleasure according to their desire.

13- Thus the community is now confined to all temporal affections. He fills himself with unrestrained gluttony and the vanity of the world. He completes without reason the pleasure of his flesh.

14- But although my enemies are many, yet among them I have many friends, however secret. As it was said to Helias, who thought that no friend of mine would survive but himself: 'I have,' said he, 'seven thousand men who have not bowed their knees before Baal,' so I, though there are many enemies, yet have secret friends among them. who weep every day, because my enemies have exalted themselves, and because my name is despised.

15- Therefore, because of their prayers, just as a charitable and good king, knowing the evil deeds of the city, patiently tolerates the inhabitants and sends letters to his friends, making them wary of their danger, so I send my words to my friends, who are not so obscure as the Apocalypse, which I was shown to John under darkness, that they might be explained by my spirit in his time, when it pleased me.

16- Nor are they so secret that they are not announced - as Paul saw of my mysteries, which it was not permitted to speak - but they are so open that all, both small and great, understand them, so light that all who wish can grasp them.

17- Therefore, let my friends make my words come to my enemies, if by chance they are converted, and let them know their danger and judgment, so that they may repent of their deeds!

18- Otherwise, it will be the judgment of the city, and just as a wall is interrupted, where no stone is left on top of a stone, and in the foundation two stones will not adhere to each other, so it will happen to the city, that is, to the world.

19- But the judges will burn with the most burning fire. But no fire is more burning than that which is nourished by some fat.

20- These judges were fat, because they had more opportunity to fulfill their will, they exceeded others in honor and temporal abundance, they abounded in malice and iniquity more than others. Therefore they will burn in a very hot pan.

21- The defenders will be hanged on the highest gallows. For the gallows consist of two upright timbers and a third placed transversely as a threshold.

22- This gallows with two sticks is their very own pen, which consists of two sticks. First, because they did not expect my eternal premium and did not work for it.

23- The second thing is that they distrusted my power and goodness, that I could not and would not give them everything to be sufficient.

24- But the wood is from the transversal of their conscience, namely, from the fact that they understood well and did evil and were not ashamed to do it against their conscience.

25- But the rope of the gallows is an eternal fire, which is not quenched by water, nor is it cut by tongs, nor is it terminated or broken by age.

26- In these gallows, where there is a severe punishment and an unquenchable fire, they will hang and have confusion like traitors.

27- They will feel miseries, because they were faithless. They will hear reproaches, because my words displeased them. Woe will be in their mouth, because praise and honor were sweet to them.

28- In these gallows they will tear them alive, that is, the demons, who are never satisfied. But even those who are torn are not consumed: the tortured live without end, and the tormentors live without end.

29- There will be woe that will never end, misery that will never be alleviated. Woe unto them that were ever born! Woe to them, because their lives had been prolonged!

30- Thirdly, the justice of laborers is like that of bulls. Bulls have very hard flesh and skin. Therefore, their judgment is the sharpest blade. This sharp iron is the death of hell, which will torment those who despised me and loved their own will instead of my commandment.

31- Therefore the letter, that is, my words, was written. Let my friends work hard to come to my enemies wisely and discreetly, if perhaps they will listen and repent.

32- But if some, hearing my words, should say: 'Let us wait a little while longer, the time has not yet come, it is not yet his time', I swear by my deity that Adam was driven out of paradise, he sent Pharaoh ten plagues, that I am coming to them sooner than they believe;

33- I swear by my humanity, which I took from a virgin without sin for the salvation of men, in which I had tribulation in my heart, I suffered punishment in the flesh, death for the life of men, in which I rose and ascended and sit at the right hand of the Father, true God and man in one person, that I will complete my words;

34- I swear by my Spirit, who was sent upon the apostles on the day of Pentecost and incited them to speak in the tongues of all nations, that unless they return to me with correction as if they were weak and feeble, I will take vengeance on them in my wrath.

35- Then woe will be to them in body and in soul. Alas, because the living came into the world and lived in the world. Alas, because their pleasure was small and still vain, and their torment will be perpetual.

36- Then they will understand what they now disdain to believe, that my words were of charity. Then they should understand that I warned them like a father and they refused to listen to me.

37- Behold, if they will not believe the words of kindness, they will believe the works when they come."

Chapter 57

The words of the Lord to the bride, how he himself is in the souls of Christians abhorrent and despised food, and on the contrary the world is delightful and beloved in them, and about the terrible judgment brought against such.

1- The son spoke to the bride: "So do the Christians to me now, just as the Jews did to me. They threw me out of the temple and had the perfect will to kill me, but because my hour had not yet come, I escaped from their hands.

2- So the Christians are doing to me now. They cast me out from their temple, that is, from their soul, which ought to be my temple, and they would gladly kill me if they could.

3- I am in their mouth like rotting and stinking flesh, and I appear to them as a man speaking lies, and they care nothing about me. They turn their backs to me, and I turn my back to them, because there is nothing in their mouths but lust, and in their flesh lust like cattle. In the hearing of them only pride pleases, in the sight of the pleasures of the world.

4- But my passion and my charity are abominable to them, and my life is high.

5- Therefore I will do as that animal does, which has many hiding places: when it is pursued by hunters in one hiding place, it flees to another. I will do so, because the Christians persecute me with their evil works and cast me out of the secret place of their hearts.

6- Therefore I want to go to the Gentiles, in whose mouth I am now bitter and insipid, and in their mouth I will be sweeter than honey. However, I am still so merciful that whoever has sinned will be forgiven and will say: 'Lord, I know that I have sinned grievously and I gladly want to make amends through your grace. Pity me because of your bitter passion!', I gladly received him.

7- But those who persist in their evil, I will forgive them like a giant, who has three things, namely, terribleness, strength and roughness.

8- So I will forgive the terrible Christians, so that they dare not move the least finger against me. I will come and be so strong that they will be like gnats before me. Thirdly, I will forgive them so harshly, that they will feel woe in the present and woe without end.

Chapter 58

The words of the Mother to the bride and of the Mother and the Son sweetly united and how unjust Christ is bitter, bitterer and bitterest and sweeter and sweeter than the good ones.

1- The mother spoke to the bride: "Consider, new bride, the passion of my son, whose passion surpassed the passion of all the saints in bitterness. For just as a mother, if she saw her son cut alive, would be most bitterly troubled, so I was troubled by the bitterness of my son's suffering."

2- Then he spoke to his son: "Blessed are you, my son, because you are holy, as it is sung: 'Holy, holy, holy Lord God of Sabaoth.' Blessed are you, because you are sweet, sweeter and sweetest!

3- You were holy before the incarnation, holy in the womb, holy after the incarnation. You were also sweet before the creation of the world, sweeter than the angels, sweetest to me in the incarnation."

4- The son answered: "Blessed are you, mother, before all the angels! For just as I was the sweetest to you, as you said just now, so I am bitter, more bitter, most bitter to the evil ones.

5- I am bitter to those who say that I created many things without a cause, who blaspheme that I created man for death, not for life. O wretched and senseless thought!

6- Did I, the most just and virtuous, create the angels without reason? Would I have enriched man with so much goodness, if I had created him for damnation? No way.

7- For I have done all things well, and out of love I have given every good thing to man. But he himself turns all good things into evil for himself, not because I have done anything evil, but because man himself, when he is otherwise bound according to the divine constitution, moves his will. This is bad.

8- But I am more bitter than those who say that I have given myself free will to sin and not to do good, who say that I am unjust because I harm others and justify others, who impute to me that they are evil because I withdraw grace from them.

9- But I am most bitter towards those who say that my law and commandments are very difficult and that no one can fulfill them, who say that my passion is of no value to them. For this reason they regard it as nothing.

10- Therefore, I swear on my life, as I once swore to the prophets, that I will excuse myself before the angels and all my saints, and these, to whom I am bitter, will prove that I created all things rationally and well, and that not even the smallest worm exists without a cause for the benefit and education of man.

11- But those who love me more will prove that I wisely gave free will for the good of man. They will also know that I am just, who gives to the good man an eternal kingdom, but to the evil man punishment.

12- For it was not fitting for the devil, who was made good by me and fell from his malice, to have company with the good. They will also prove that bad people are not because of my fault, because they are bad but because of their own fault.

13- For I, if it were possible, would willingly accept such a penalty for each person as I once received on the cross for all, so that they might return to the promised inheritance.

14- But man always has his will contrary to mine. I therefore gave him liberty, that he might serve me, if he pleased, and that he might have an eternal premium. But if he would not, he would have to be punished with the devil, because of whose malice and his followers hell was justly made.

15- For I, because I am charitable, do not want a man to obey me out of fear or under compulsion, like an irrational animal, but out of divine charity, because no one can see my face who secretly obeys me or almost out of fear.

16- Those, however, to whom I am most bitter, will understand in their conscience that my law was the lightest and my yoke the softest, and they will grieve inconsolably because they despised my law and because they loved more the world, whose yoke is much heavier and more difficult than mine."

17- Then the mother answered: "Blessed are you, my son, my God and my Lord! I beg you, that because you were the sweetest to me, others may share in my sweetness."

18- To whom the son answered: "Blessed are you, dearest mother! Your words are sweet and full of love. Therefore, whoever receives your sweetness in his mouth and holds it perfectly, he will prosper."

19- But he who receives and rejects will have a much more bitter punishment." Then answered the Virgin: "Blessed are you, my son, for all your love!"

Chapter 59

The words of Christ present to the bride, that is to say, how Christ is designated and represented by the peasant, good priests by the good shepherd, bad priests by the bad shepherd, and good Christians by the wife. In which shape many useful things are contained.

1- I am the one who never said anything wrong. I am considered in the world as a peasant, whose name seems to be despised. My words are considered foolish and my house is considered a cheap hut.

2- This peasant had a wife whom he wanted nothing but according to his will, who possessed everything with her husband and had him as her master, obeying him in everything as her master.

3- This peasant also had many sheep, for the keeping of which he hired a shepherd for five golds, and to attend to the necessities of his life.

4- This shepherd, because he was a good man, used gold for his own benefit, and vines for food when necessary.

5- After this shepherd, passing at some time, another worse man came, who bought himself a wife with gold, to whom he brought his provisions, resting continually with her, not caring about the sheep, which were miserably scattered by the cruel beasts.

6- Then the peasant, seeing the dispersion of his sheep, cried out, saying: 'My shepherd is unfaithful to me. My eggs were scattered and devoured by the most ferocious beasts.

7- Then the wife said to the peasant, her husband: 'My lord, the bodies that have been devoured, it is certain that we shall not recover them. Therefore, those bodies which remain untouched, even though they are without spirit, let us bring them home and use them! For if we were to avoid it altogether, it would be intolerable to us.'

8- The husband answered her: 'What shall we do then? Because the animals were poisoned with their teeth, the flesh of the ouia was similarly infected with deadly poison, the skin was corrupted, and the wool was gathered together.'

9- The wife answered: 'If everything is stained and everything is taken away, where will we live?'

10- The husband answered: 'I see ewes living in three places. There are some who are like dead eggs, who dare not breathe for fear. Secondly, they lie in deep mud, and are not able to extricate themselves. Thirdly, they stand in hiding and do not dare to proceed.

11- Therefore, my wife, come and let us raise the eggs that are trying to rise and without help are not enough, and let us use them!

12- Behold, I, the Lord, am that peasant, because I am considered by men as a donkey fed in its bed according to its manner and manners. My name is a holy disposition of the Church.

13- This is considered contemptible, because the sacraments of the Church, namely, baptism, confirmation, unction, penance, and marriage, are received as if in derision and given to others because of greed.

14- My words are judged foolish, because the words which I spoke with my own mouth with similes, are turned from spiritual intelligence to the alleviation of the body.

15- My house seems to be despised, because earthly things are loved instead of heavenly ones.

16- By that first pastor, whom I had, I understood my friends, that is, the priests, whom I once had in the holy Church, because by the term of one I understand many. To these I committed my vows, that is, to sanctify my most worthy body, and to govern and defend the souls of my elect.

17- I also gave them five goods, more precious than all gold, namely, an intelligent conscience above all irrational things, so that they could distinguish between good and evil, between truth and falsity.

18- Secondly, I gave them intelligence and wisdom of spiritual things; which is now forgotten and is loved for that human wisdom.

19- Thirdly, I gave them chastity, fourthly, moderation in all things and abstinence in bodily control, fifthly, stability in good manners, words and deeds.

20- After this first pastor, that is, my friends, who were in my church of old, other wicked pastors now entered, who bought themselves a wife for gold, that is, for chastity, and for those five goods they assumed a female body, that is, incontinence, because of which my spirit departed from them

21- For when they have a complete will to sin and satiate their spouse, that is, their pleasure at will, then my spirit is absent from them, because they do not care about the harm of others, if they can complete their will.

22- Now those who are completely devoted are those whose souls are in hell and whose bodies are buried in the graves awaiting the resurrection of eternal damnation.

23- But those whose flesh remains and whose spirit has been taken away are those who neither love nor fear me, nor are they affected by any devotion or concern around me.

24- For my spirit is far from them, because their flesh is poisoned by the poisonous teeth of beasts, that is, their soul and thoughts, which are marked in the flesh of the udders and intestines, are so bitter to me and abominable to delight in them as flesh is poisoned.

25- Their skin, that is, their body, is dry from all good and from all charity and fit for no use in my kingdom, but will be delivered to the eternal fire in hell after judgment.

26- Their wool, that is, their works, are so completely useless that nothing is found in them for which they are worthy to have my charity and grace.

27- What shall we do now, O my wife, that is, good Christians, whom I understand by wife? I see living eggs in three places. There are some who are like dead eggs, who dare not breathe for fear.

28- These are the Gentiles, who would gladly have the right faith, if they knew how. But they themselves do not dare to breathe, that is, they do not dare to let go of the faith they have for fear, and they do not dare to receive the right one.

29- Secondly, there are those who stand in hiding and do not dare to proceed. Here are the Jews who stand as if under a veil. They would gladly proceed, if they knew for certain that I was born.

30- But they hide themselves, as it were, under a veil, because in the figures and signs which signified me in the law and were truly completed in me, they hope for salvation, and from that vain hope they fear to proceed to the right faith.

31- A third of the ewes that stand in the mud are Christians, established in mortal sins. For they themselves would willingly rise for fear of execution, but they cannot because of grave sins and because they have no charity.

32- Therefore, my wife, that is, good Christians, help me! For as a wife and husband are bound to be one flesh and one member, so the Christian is my member and I his, because I am in him and he is in me.

33- Therefore, O wife, that is to say, good Christians, run with me to the sheep that still have spirit, and let us raise them up and restore them! Take pity on me, because I bought a lot of eggs! Get back with me and I with you, you on the back and I on the head!

34- I gladly take them between my hands. I carried them all once on my back, when it was all butchered and attached to a log.

35- O my friends, I so love to hold on to these vows, that if it were possible for me to die for any of them by a special death, such as I suffered once on the cross for all, I would rather redeem them than lose them.

36- Therefore, I cry to my friends with all my heart, that they spare no effort for me, not good ones, and if I was not spared from words of abuse while I was in the world, they will not spare themselves to speak the truth about me.

37- I was not ashamed of that contemptible death for them. As I was born, I stood naked before the eyes of my enemies. I was struck with a fist in the teeth, I was pulled by the hair with their fingers, I was scourged with their whips, I was fastened to a tree with their instruments and hung with thieves and robbers on the cross.

38- Therefore, my friends, do not spare yourself from laboring for me, who endured such things out of charity for your sake! Work hard and help those in need!

39- I swear by my humanity, which is in the Father, and the Father in me, and by the deity, which is in my Spirit, and the Spirit in it, and the same Spirit in me, and I in it, and these three are one God in three persons, that whoever has labored and carried my burdens with me, I will meet them in the middle of the road to help them and I will give them the most precious reward, that is, myself, for eternal joy."

Chapter 60

The words of the Son to the bride about the three types of Christians, represented by the Jews existing in Egypt, and how these were revealed to the bride to be transferred and witnessed and preached by the friends of God to ignorant persons.

1- The son spoke to the bride, saying: "I am the God of Israel and he who spoke with Moses. Moses, when he was sent to my people, did some sign, saying: 'The people do not believe me otherwise.'

2- If, then, it was the Lord's people to whom Moses was sent, why did he distrust it? But you must know that there were three kinds of people among those people.

3- Some believed in God and Moses. The second group were those who believed in God and distrusted Moses, considering that he might not presume to speak or do such things out of his own consent and presumption. There were third parties who believed neither in God nor in Moses.

4- If now there are three kinds of men among Christians, who are marked in Hebrews. There are some who believe well in God and in my words. There are others who believe in God but distrust my words, because they do not know how to distinguish between a good spirit and an evil spirit. There are third parties who believe neither me nor you, with whom I have spoken my words.

5- But, as I said, although some of the Hebrews distrusted Moses, they all crossed the Red Sea with him into the hermitage, where those who distrusted worshiped idols and provoked God to anger. Therefore, they were consumed by a miserable death, but they did this only to those who had bad faith.

6- Therefore, because the human mind is slow to believe, my friend will translate my words to those who believe him. They later spread it to others who do not know how to distinguish between a good spirit and an evil one.

7- And if the hearers receive a sign, let them show them the staff, as Moses did, that is, let them explain my words to them. For as the rod of Moses was straight and terrible because of its transformation into a serpent, so my words are straight, so that no falsehood is found in them.

8- They are terrible, because they sound like a righteous judgment. They propose and bear witness that at the word and sound of one mouth the devil yielded and withdrew from God's creation, who, if he were not restrained by my power, could even move mountains.

9- What then was the power of him, with the permission of God, who fled at the sound of a single voice? Therefore, just as those Hebrews, who neither believed in God nor Moses, went out of Egypt into the land of promise as if by joining others, so now many Christians will go with my chosen ones as if they were strangers, because they do not trust in my power, that I can save them.

10- Insofar as they do not believe in my words, they have a false hope in my virtue. However, my words will be fulfilled without their will, and as if they are warming themselves to perfection, until they come to a place that pleases me."

The Scriptorium Project is the work of a small group of lay people of various apostolic churches who are interested in the preservation, transmission, and translation of the works of the early and medieval church. Our efforts are to make the works of the church fathers accessible to anyone who might have an interest in Christian antiquities and the theological, philosophical, and moral writings that have become the bedrock of Western Civilization.

To-date, our releases have pulled from the Greek, Syriac, Georgian, Latin, Celtic, Ethiopian, and Coptic traditions of Christianity, and have been pulled from sundry local traditions and languages.

REVELATIONS

www.ingramcontent.com/pod-product-compliance
Lightning Source LLC
LaVergne TN
LVHW061035070526
838201LV00073B/5038